THE WAY U'S WERE
A Personal History of Colchester United

THE WAY U'S WERE
A Personal History of Colchester United

TEMPUS

First published 2004

Tempus Publishing Limited
The Mill, Brimscombe Port,
Stroud, Gloucestershire, GL5 2QG
www.tempus-publishing.com

© Bernard Webber, 2004

The right of Bernard Webber to be identified as the Author
of this work has been asserted in accordance with the
Copyrights, Designs and Patents Act 1988.

British Library Cataloguing in Publication Data.
A catalogue record for this book is available from the British Library.

ISBN 0 7524 3119 6

Typesetting and origination by Tempus Publishing Limited
Printed in Great Britain

Contents

About the Author

Bernard Webber has a been a sports journalist since the 1940s, starting his career with the old-style *Essex County Telegraph* broadsheet. He later joined the *Essex County Standard* and the weekly *Colchester Gazette* and, after spells with the *Worcester Evening News* and *Manchester City News,* teamed up again with the *County Telegraph,* then a bright tabloid, as Sports Editor.

When the *Telegraph* folded he became associated with the *Essex Chronicle* series of newspapers based at Chelmsford, eventually as overall Sports Editor. The other titles included the *Colchester Express* which he helped to launch, and *Brentwood Gazette.* For a number of years, the *Express* developed into one of the best ever Colchester sports-orientated papers.

Bernard Webber took an early retirement and has since operated as a successful soccer and cricket freelance journalist, contributing to many nationals and leading provincials, also working for Anglia Television, and broadcasting for radio stations up and down the country. For two years, he was editor of the then well-known Colchester free sheet, *The Leader*, and through the years has frequently been the Colchester United Programme Editor.

Bernard Webber's life-long cricketing journalistic career was marked in 1995 when he was made an honorary life member of the Essex County Cricket Club.

Introduction

I have had the idea for this book for some while. There have been some previous excellent Colchester United publications but these have concentrated largely on statistics. My aim has been to recapture soccer as it was in arguably more romantic eras. Previously, when money was not the predominant factor, and life and sport were generally more laid-back and carefree, we had a largely untroubled game on and off the field.

Watching and following Colchester United was and remains a habit. Supporters sit and stand in the same spot match by match. They have their favourite players, past and present, and their own particular memories of games, managers and performers down the years.

In these pages, I have attempted to bring them back to life and vividly restore another soccer era. There are also a host of interesting behind-the-scenes stories from the birth of the club right through to the current Phil Parkinson era.

I must thank my wife, daughter, son-in-law and granddaughters Rebecca and Maddy for their help and patience in computer problems and the assistance of Bob Jackson, Dick Graham, Frances Ponder who kindly loaned several photographs. I would also like to acknowledge Headline Books for extracts from *The Way It Was* by Stanley Matthews.

Last but by no means least, I give sincere thanks to my old friend, Ernest Jenkins, without whose persistent encouragement *The Way U's Were* would never have been written.

1
On the Map

Giant-Killers

Soccer in the late 1940s was part of the golden age. Then it could truthfully be called the 'beautiful game'. Superstar legends like Stanley Matthews, Raich Carter and Tom Finney were parading and at their peak. The post-war boom was still flourishing. The Second World War remained very much in people's minds and having suffered a starvation diet of ersatz soccer, they flocked to matches and crowds were enormous.

There were no red or yellow cards, no substitutes, no floodlights and no penalty shoot-outs. Most significantly, there was practically no violence. As a consequence, there was no need for crowd segregation.

On this fascinating stage Southern League minnows Colchester United left their own indelible mark. It was 1947/48, and they revelled in an FA Cup run that saw them defeat in turn Chelmsford City, Banbury Spencer and League clubs Wrexham, Huddersfield Town and Bradford Park Avenue.

Amazingly, Colchester United reached the fifth round and it took Blackpool and Matthews to end it all, Blackpool going on to the final where they lost to Manchester United in what has always been regarded as a Wembley classic.

Colchester players were almost completely part-time and a lot of the players trained away from Layer Road, yet they became the most talked about team in the country and shared the headlines with the top clubs.

The Cup run was little short of sensational. Wrexham were a powerful Third Division outfit and Huddersfield were in First Division in the same way as today's Premiership and Bradford Park Avenue were Second Division material and created a sensation of their own by knocking out mighty Arsenal at Highbury. Later Bradford became defunct but there is still a team named Bradford PA operating in the Unibond League.

For years, West Ham United's well-known defender, Ted Fenton, was Colchester's player-manager. He was the frontman from every aspect and ran the club single-handedly from his office – a nondescript hut in a corner of the ground. Fenton had Colchester connections having appeared for the old Town amateur side in the early 1930s. Now at thirty-five years old, he was back playing as well as ever.

The players called Fenton 'The Governor' and he was a born leader – tall, debonair, a snazzy dresser, and always smoking his pipe. He recruited well and hand-picked his players. Five of the players were war heroes and it must be remembered that the great conflict was only a recent memory. Rationing remained a chore and many other restrictions were in force.

The five war heroes were: Harry Bearryman, a good-looking classy wing half from Chelsea, who had been a crew member of an RAF bomber that frequently raided Berlin; skipper Bob Curry, an inspirational forward who became a U's legend – as a soldier, he had been injured at Dunkirk and was told he would never play football again; right-winger Dennis Hillman, who had been a commando although you would never have imagined it when you saw him sportingly dressed in plus fours; striker Fred Cutting, who had been in the Scots Guards and won the Military Medal for bravery in action; and centre forward Arthur Turner, had been shot down when an RAF warrant officer – he spent days in an open boat before being rescued.

So plenty of wartime spirit prevailed and while they didn't set the Southern League alight, the team gelled well and were utterly inspired when it came to cup ties. The players were lionised and fêted wherever they went. Layer Road games were well patronised, every match seeming a big occasion. It was as if these happy band of supporters were hell-bent on making up for those austere wartime years.

The goalkeeper was handsome Harry Wright, an imposing figure. He had been in top-grade football with Charlton and Derby and proved a great shot-stopper. But, it must be said, he was suspect on crosses.

The backs were Albert Kettle and Bob Allen. Kettle was only 5ft 5in tall, but a terrier-like tackler and a dynamic performer. He was an Eight Ash Green lad and being local, the crowd loved him, nicknaming him 'Digger'. Allen, who had been with Northampton and Brentford was, by comparison, tall and studious. Like Wright, he was a PT instructor.

Bearryman, Fenton and Andy Brown were the middle line; Brown being a dour Scot was both industrious and a good ball distributor.

Hillman, Curry, Turner and Cutting, the war heroes, were joined by left-winger Len Cater, an amateur who had won several Essex county caps and played for the old Colchester Town side before the war. He was in some ways the most improbable of all the giant-killers. A gas fitter by trade, Len was short and stocky but made up for his stature with a brash confidence. He was a wonderful crosser of the ball.

Another rather improbable player was Turner for he should, by all rights, still have been playing First Division football. He was an amateur in a Cup final when he led the Charlton Athletic attack against Derby County in the 1945/46 Wembley showpiece. It was odd that he should drop into the non-League ranks against the likes of Exeter Reserves, and even stranger that he turned professional thanks, one imagines, to the glib persuasive tongue of Fenton — it was no secret that Turner was on top money. Also ironic was that Charlton returned to Wembley without him and were then winners against Burnley. Turner, a cheery character, thoroughly enjoyed his football and was highly popular. He worked in his father's timber business and was a skilled ball-playing type of striker. He carried on at Layer Road right into their League baptism season of 1950/51.

It was difficult to imagine that when the great conflict was raging only a few years earlier, Turner had languished for hours in an open boat in the English Channel, and the cool, calm and collected Bearryman had flown through anti-aircraft flak over burning Berlin.

The cornerstone of the Colchester giant-killers was, without doubt, Fenton. He had vast experience in the Second Division and was in the England touring party to South Africa in 1939.

He commanded in the air and passed the ball well. There was an attacking air about his play and he scored the occasional goal. But above all else, he was a born leader, a splendid organiser, and a fantastic showman all rolled into one.

Ted had been an aristocrat member of the pre-war West Ham team, which had the reputation of a soccer academy of arts, including the likes of that bow-legged inside forward genius Len Goulden, and others such as Archie Macaulay, Stan Foxall and Jackie Morton. They all played in that very odd first wartime Wembley cup final when the Hammers beat Blackburn Rovers in June 1940. It was strange and unreal in that there were 42,000 people making up the crowd, and the game was played out against the background of world-shattering events on the Dunkirk beaches, one of the biggest crisis points of the conflict. So Ted won his medal about the same time as the injured Bob Curry was being shipped back to England.

At Upton Park, Fenton mostly performed at wing half but at Layer Road, he was the central defender, a role he played with a great deal of panache. He had a sort of superior disdain to opponents in the area that he commanded so efficiently.

Fenton's first season was 1946/47 and he missed only three games. Curry, Turner, Hillman and Cater also made their bows but nothing was won with an eighth position achieved and there was a five-goal rout at Reading in the FA Cup.

The following season, which was to produce the memorable giant-killing run, started with a goal glut and an amazing 11,419 gate saw Gloucester City walloped 8-0. The fresh-faced Hillman, who scored a fair number of goals, registered a hat-trick – one of the few I remember coming from a winger.

That crowd, for just a bread and butter Southern League game, was extraordinary, but Colchester was in the grip of post-war soccer fever and support came from a wide outlaying area. The thriving supporters club had flourishing enthusiastic branches in neighbouring towns and villages.

Those big crowds were impeccably behaved, and I recall the packed Spion Kop end needed the attention of only one policeman – burly and helmeted of course!

The cup run started in the fourth qualifying round with a comfortable 3-1 home win over rivals Chelmsford City who, although not at their best about this time, always pulled in a good crowd, over 10,000 in this case. Goals by Curry (2), and Turner saw U's enthusiasm building.

At the first-round stage, Banbury Spencer, a little-known works team from the Birmingham League, presented a much tougher struggle.

Banbury might have looked something of a circus act with their over-the-top multi-coloured shirts that caused much amusement, but they were no joke when they took the lead. United were clearly not at their best and it was close to half-time when Brown came up with one of his rare goals to level. Then Curry bundled home the winner, knocking himself out in the process after Cater had hit a post. Curry always maintained it was the hardest match of the entire run.

The campaign had begun with a stripling of a lad, Vic Keeble, making his bow in the opening game against Bedford, scoring a hat-trick. He was destined for stardom but never figured in the Cup-run side which was unchanged apart from Edgar Williams deputising for the injured Hillman against Banbury. Neither did Frank Rist or well-known forwards Ian Gillespie and Alf Biggs get a look in.

After the first-round scare, it was home again to face League opposition for the first time. They played against Wrexham of the Third Division (North), a redoubtable top-ranking side who in fact finished just outside the promotion frame at the season's end.

There were nearly 11,000 people making up the crowd for this thriller: a match full of twists and turns and two missed penalty kicks. The hotly-contested affair had hung in the balance until the 72nd minute, when a vintage Curry header broke the deadlock after Turner had veered to the right and delivered a perfect cross.

About ten minutes later, we had the big talking point. Wrexham's left-winger, the ever-menacing Bill Tunnicliffe, who had earlier hit the wood-work, was sent sprawling by Kettle as he closed in on the goal. It was a clear penalty but Tunnicliffe had been injured in the process and, while he was receiving lengthy treatment, goalkeeper Wright indulged in some blatant gamesmanship.

Unseen by the referee, but spotted by many hawk-eyed spectators, Wright slyly buried the ball deep on the muddy penalty spot. Eventually Tunnicliffe recovered but declined to take the kick – he was the regular penalty man – and Boothway stepped up instead, and half hit his shot straight at Wright!

Later, in a dramatic finale, United also had a penalty but Turner's kick was brilliantly saved so Curry' goal proved enough. He was a Geordie who had been with Gainsborough Trinity and Sheffield Wednesday. There was no way back to Hillsborough so Fenton nipped in to take a chance with a player whose shoulder injury threatened his career. Curry went on to become a legend and was still a star when Colchester broke into the League in 1950.

The victory over Wrexham brought useful national publicity. These were heady days and the pilgrimage to Layer Road was, for many, a case of walking or cycling. The mass car age was a long way off and a shuttle bus service from the town centre was well patronised.

Look at pictures of the time and you will observe that most men wore trilby hats or caps which were all the vogue. They were a happy band of brothers, and when Colchester scored, many an eternal friendship was struck by total strangers.

What was amazing was the fact that United comprised only four full-timers and Fenton had to take on trust the majority who were scattered far and wide and carried out their own training programmes.

One must remember too that apart from Fenton and goalkeeper Wright, the players had little full League experience and Bearryman had never played for Chelsea's first team.

The cup-tie fever grew when the third-round draw decreed Huddersfield Town were to come to Layer Road. Fenton had new gimmicks to exploit, immediately formulating an F-plan diet and the players began to train on oysters.

The problem now would be to accommodate the crowd. There had been 11,000 people for Wrexham, but a 16,000 limit was agreed for Huddersfield – and to pack those numbers into the tiny tree-fringed ground would be no easy feat.

Even in those days, the police were very safety conscious and after inspections, it was agreed that there would be two more entrance points, and concrete blocks on the Spion Kop had to be strengthened. By today's standards, 16,000 was a remarkably high figure and the seating was limited. So all was set for the next epic Cup tie and what a sensation was in store.

Red-Hot Curry

Huddersfield came to Layer Road for the third round as firm favourites, even though they were in the lower regions of the First Division. They boasted a great Cup tradition and had the famed flame-haired Irish international inside forward Peter Doherty. Today, the First Division is the Premiership and in those days was just as glamorous and star-studded.

Huddersfield had been 1922 Cup winners and finalists four times. In the 1920s, they were First Division Champions three seasons in succession and a member of that side, Clem Stephenson, was manager. They were a club steeped in history, so imagine the excitement of their visit to little old Layer Road, hosting a big-time club for the first time ever.

How would the renowned Doherty, owning a sackful of Irish caps, cope with the tiny cramped ground as compared with the vast Leeds Road arena that accommodated 60,000 people and which is now no more (a supermarket having been built on the site)?

Doherty, although in the veteran stage, was still a prince among inside forwards and only two years earlier had been an FA Cup winner with Derby County who beat Charlton Athletic 4-1. Doherty too, playing alongside the great Raich Carter, had been on the scoresheet. Pre-war, he had been with Manchester City and in the famous sky-blue shirt been featured in the many cigarette card issues of the day.

Huddersfield were far from being a one-man team. Other names from pre-war days were goalkeeper Bob Hesford, full-back Bill Hayes and midfielder Eddie Boot. Hesford and Boot featured in the Wembley side beaten by Preston in the 1937/38 cup final. This was the famous game in which a George Mutch penalty decided the issue in the last minute of extra time. Hesford, a bachelor of arts, 6ft plus and an imposing figure, would for sure always remember that dramatic moment as he would the crucial 70th minute of the match against the so-called Colchester minnows.

Of the up-and-coming brigade, Huddersfield had much-vaunted left-winger Vic Metcalfe who everyone raved about, as well as the skilled Jimmy Glazzard. Both later earned England caps and, all in all, the Town team was a formidable blend of experience and youth.

The day of the match, Saturday 10 January 1948, dawned bright, and Huddersfield supporters travelling through the night arrived early. It had been a twelve-hour journey and many were still asleep, wrapped in their rugs and blankets. Red favours were sported for Town's blue and white striped shirts clashed with U's. Colchester adopted the colours when turning professional in 1937 – manager Ted Davis had been a former player with the Yorkshire club. For the big game, Colchester sported claret and blue – West Ham's strip and Fenton's idea, you could bet.

These hardy Yorkshire folk weaned on a diet of quality soccer expected it to be a pushover. They came with their own mascot to vie with Colchester's Harry Fosker, the umbrella man who always ran out with the team. One could never fathom out the significance of the umbrella but it was all harmless fun with never the hint of crowd trouble. Plenty of good-humoured banter but certainly no violence. The souvenir programme, a flimsy effort, was priced sixpence and eagerly snapped up.

The gates opened early and by 1 p.m. 16,000 people were somehow jammed in, clinging to the rafters, so to speak: some in trees, others on the roofs of the stands. The air was full of high expectancy and woodbine smoke and the contest started with a minor sensation as after only seconds, Doherty received the ball full in his face and was laid out!

He recovered, but in hindsight I often wonder if he suffered concussion. Truth was that as the game progressed, the commanding Fenton and brilliant Harry Bearryman completely blotted him out. The man expected to be a key figure was seldom a factor.

Colchester played out of their skins, set the pace, and harried and bustled their opponents at every turn. Dennis Hillman outshone Metcalfe, and Arthur Turner, with a series of controlled dribbles, caused all sorts of consternation. This was the Turner who had played against Doherty at Wembley in 1946 and he looked a world-beater. In fact, there was a constant audacious touch and little Fred Cutting came up with a cheeky solo past four defenders.

At half-time Colchester had had the edge and Fenton said in the dressing room, 'You've got them rattled now go out and win' – and so they did.

Huddersfield's £50,000-rated side were indeed totally upset by fierce tackling, the narrowness of the pitch, and the crowd breathing down their necks. Hayes and Boot, who were in the veteran stage, also found the pace a little too hot.

For the umpteenth time, Turner had Hesford desperately saving before the memorable 70th minute and the winning goal still etched indelibly in the mind. Kettle made the most remarkable of runs deep from defence. He was the smallest player in the action but, roared on by a crescendo of noise, went on and on, a trail of opponents in his wake. Finally, on the edge of the box, he was hacked down by Conway Smith.

The free-kick by studious Bob Allen pierced the defensive wall, Hesford could only partly save and Bob Curry did the rest. Amid utter pandemonium, he calmly transferred the spinning ball from one foot to the other and, ice cool, picked his spot.

For those who attach great importance from such facts, the goal – arguably one of the most historic of them all – was at the so-called favoured Layer Road end.

The last twenty minutes were played out to a continuous roar. A late Huddersfield rally was snuffed out and U's sailed to victory – each player chaired off at the end, and the crowd shouting for Fenton, who duly appeared with an appropriate little speech.

Huddersfield took their shock defeat sportingly and at a town hall reception, a smiling Doherty was pictured with hero of the day, Curry. Town boss Stephenson admitted that Colchester were the better side on the day, while a director said 'Beat another First Division side and we can hold up our heads again.'

A jubilant Fenton, who tactically was something of an Alf Ramsey of the 1940s, told of his 'F-plan' which involved the opposition defence. Fenton claimed the left-back was one-footed, so Hillman had to practice going one way to draw him off position, while Turner kept dribbling the ball along the ground. All this and Ted's lucky champagne cork, kept in his shorts, was seized on by the national press who were having a field day.

The shock win was highly acclaimed and the *Daily Express* produced a diagram showing in detail how the goal arrived. Frank Butler, one of the top writers of the day said, 'Remember Walsall's sensational defeat of Arsenal. The taming of Huddersfield by non-League Colchester was greater.'

W.J. Hicks of the *News Chronicle* penned 'The collapse of a First Division cup prospect against a team whose normal opposition is from Exeter Reserves, Barry and the like was not accidental. They were the better team on the day.'

But the words I liked best were Alan Everett's in the local *County Telegraph*. He wrote, 'The secret trial, the oyster diet and even the famous champagne cork may have had something to do with the win. I wouldn't know but I suggest it was something a good deal more tangible that brought about one of the biggest upsets in football history and that was the fact that Ted Fenton cannot visualise any opposition too strong for his team and manages to imbue the same spirit into the side which is making football history.'

The players basked in the media spotlight and were photographed at home with their families. Enquiries from League clubs began to come in, Huddersfield themselves asking about Kettle and Bearryman. Curry, the golden-goal man, was also on wanted lists. One cannot overemphasise what a superb forward he was, perfect control and balance and one of the game's thinkers. It was an age of superstars and Bob could have been up there alongside them in the top divisions.

The day after the Huddersfield tie, national papers continued to pester Ted Fenton in his house in All Saints Avenue, and Curry was photographed on the treatment table for an ankle injury. Turner and goal-keeper Wright were also nursing injuries.

At the ground on Sunday there was a scene almost resembling enemy war action. The vast 16,000 crowd had left behind a lot of damage. Some sleepers had been bodily lifted out and piled up at the back. One supposes, in hindsight, that it was miraculous there had been no crowd trouble or injury. Certainly it was something that could never happen today.

There was a fascinating event recently when five young girl supporters met up for the opening game of the 2002/03 season against Stockport County. In 1948, they attended the Colchester High School for Girls and stood regularly at the Spion Kop end. Astonishingly, decades on, the five were reunited. They were Joy Davis, Ann Peaseland, Margaret Hilditch, Val Romea and Pam O 'Connell.

They chatted about the good old days for a long time. Would you believe they used to cycle to some away games and, during the summer, would knit their own scarves and jumpers ready for the soccer season? Supporters really were supporters in those days and women could safely stand on the terraces and never hear a swear word.

These were magical football days; the other games in the third round generated high excitement, and goals were plentiful. It was an age when the accent was on attack and the ultimate Wembley winners, Manchester United, beat Aston Villa 6-4 in an amazing game at Villa Park watched by a crowd of 58,683 people.

Chelsea, with Len Goulden on target, hit Barrow for 5 and Everton and Stoke were 4-goal winners away. Crowds everywhere were vast: 54,000 people at Charlton and 40,000 plus numbers at Hull. At Highbury, the attendance was 47,738 supporters for the sensational result that rivalled

Colchester's feat — the completely unfancied Bradford Park Avenue beating mighty Arsenal thanks to a Billy Elliott goal.

And would you believe, fate decreed that Bradford PA would be at Layer Road in the fourth round? It was what you call a natural — giant-killer *v.* giant-killer.

For the Huddersfield tie, the gate was the lowest of the day, but United went proudly into the fourth round boasting a unique record — they had the biggest supporters club in the country. It had more than 10,000 people, and would grow even bigger in the weeks to come.

The Cutting Edge

Bradford PA were cock-a-hoop after beating Arsenal and convinced they could put an end to the run of the cheeky non-League upstarts. Now defunct, they were solid 1948 Second Division material and superior to Third Division Bradford City who, today, are Bradford City AFC of Coca-Cola Football League One.

In 1948, Bradford played at Park Avenue, a spacious distinctive stadium they shared with Yorkshire County Cricket Club. They were prolific scorers, well-supported and colourful too with their white shirts and red, amber and black hoops. Clubs in this era stuck to their colours and many were most striking.

City had the tradition and were cup winners in 1911 but Bradford Park Avenue were riding high that season and the name on everybody's lips was Scottish winger Billy Elliott who had notched the goal that knocked out Arsenal. Another Scot was slick inside forward Johnny Downie who a year on was to be transferred to Manchester United for the then very big fee of £18,000. He replaced Johnny Morris and became a notable Busby babe.

Other well-known personalities included central defender Ron Greenwood, later to become England team manager, and ex-Leeds striker George Ainsley. All in all, they were flushed with success in unloading the mighty Gunners and it was a result that shook the football world.

By now Colchester themselves were the darlings of the entire nation and in good fettle. After much consultation, the crowd limit was raised to 17,000 people, with the introduction of ringside seating. This suggested a boxing arena with two heavyweights slugging it out. What it really meant was more intimidation for Bradford as spectators would be tight to the touchlines. I still wonder how Colchester got away with it.

Ticket demand was amazing and rapidly the game was a sell-out. Twice the number could have been sold and the busiest man was manager Fenton, who had to deal with administration, ticket sales and the training programmes. He revelled in it all and had Bradford watched to help him formulate a new F-plan.

The injury front improved when Harry Wright and Len Cater were fit again. After the Huddersfield tie, Turner, who had an injured toe, and Curry were both inactive when U's lost a Southern League cup tie at Bedford. But both played in a behind-closed-doors game between the first team and the reserves who took the part of Bradford.

Fenton predicted that Bradford would be a tougher proposition than Huddersfield who he claimed 'took it too easily'. The fans who were railway workers had no doubts, however. They scrawled messages on wagons going north proclaiming 'Bradford, you've had it chum'.

Fourth-round day, Saturday 24 January 1948, and a full-strength Colchester ran out before the packed crowd who had assembled long before the 2.45 p.m. kick-off. The atmosphere was electric and the massed ranks on the open Spion Kop end presented an amazing sight. It took one's breath away.

The game unfolded and turned out to be a classic thriller with many twists and turns. I would say it was the most gripping Layer Road game ever played, apart from the Leeds glory day.

Bradford, artisan and positive, were clearly a more menacing proposition than Huddersfield and inside twelve minutes, Elliott had scored with a floating centre cum shot that frankly Wright should have saved.

In the space of five exhilarating minutes, United were level and then dramatically in front. Attacking the Spion Kop end, they launched a series of brilliant movements. First the bouncy Cater, who really was a revelation once again, raced away, his pinpoint cross catching veteran Chick Farr in two minds and, clean as a whistle, Curry headed home.

Seconds later, Cutting, Curry and Turner were involved in a three-prong raid carried out at top speed. Curry finished off clinically at close range as the Kop went crazy. It was a picture-book First Division fashioned move and goal that should have been framed for all time.

I have a vivid recollection of gazing skywards at an array of caps and hats hurled into the air and there was a cacophony of noise from a hundred rattles. They have, of course, long since been banned.

Bradford's reply in this end-to-end thriller was to square again at 2-2 when a rare Fenton error after Jack Smith had hit the bar let in big Ainsley. The enthralling contest was in the melting pot once more and as a counter, Curry was moved to mark the menacing Elliott.

Into the second half and a sensational opening, as a Farr clearance struck Turner, rebounding into the net. Offside was given and the crowd were still buzzing from the free-kick that ensued when Kettle cleared downfield. Turner dummied and Cutting pounded straight for goal, beating the advancing Farr with a beautifully struck shot. It all happened in a flash and the crowd erupted again. Cutting's long celebratory victory run back to the centre circle was something to behold.

The remainder of the game was all tension, Bradford piling on the pressure. Often U's were glad to kick anywhere and Wright brought off some colossal saves. Colchester also had their moments, and Curry netted only to be ruled offside. Somehow they hung on in the action-packed finale to create history – the first non-Leaguers since Darlington to reach the fifth round, and that was in 1911.

Cutting's golden winner was undoubtedly his finest hour. He had a notable war record, but rarely talked about the conflict and his role in battles. Soccer and his market garden business in Norwich preoccupied him and he was a country lad at heart.

Fred had his critics and his shooting was sometimes wayward, but he was a great little battler and a rare humorist. On away journeys, his reading material was often a penny comic. Cutting's career went on into the 1950s and he made 29 League appearances, scoring 13 goals.

Considering the size of the crowd, it was amazing there were no incidents, although one spectator, W. Gale of Braintree, died of a heart attack during the second half. There were also several fainting cases but never any suggestion of crowd trouble. Plenty of banter and good-natured enthusiasm prevailed, but twice the crowd invaded the pitch – an easy business as there was then no walled perimeter. They thought the game was over, and finally when it was, the players were mobbed and Fenton carried shoulder high.

Interesting facts came to light; dynamic winger Hillman had played with his back strapped up after a kick in the kidneys. He suffered agonies from well-meaning backslapping fans; and Fenton, who had played against some of the best players in the world proclaimed, 'This is my greatest hour in sport. We have worked hard to prove ourselves worthy of League status and by our cup victory, I feel we have proved our case.'

Fenton also told of his secret plan which revolved around the Bradford full-backs playing too square. So the ploy was to keep pushing down the middle, and fittingly, all three goals came from that route. In hindsight, U's display was one of the best ever by a Colchester side. A lot of their attacking football was of First Division standard and the movement leading to Curry's second goal lives on in memory.

The celebrations were prolonged. After jubilant fans had marched en masse down Butt Road, they stayed in the rain to cheer the players who appeared on the town hall balcony with the mayor. The High Street was packed just as it was on VE Day.

The publicity that followed too was incredible. Fleet Street, then the centre of the newspaper world, went to town with glowing reports and pictures. There was also newsreel coverage in the cinemas but frankly the quality was poor. If only there had been TV cameras and video coverage. A recording of this rare thriller and great goals would have been a visual treat there for all time.

The sports writers were generous in their praise. Charles Dettmer of the *Sunday People* wrote 'It was David's day at Colchester again and another League Goliath floundered, this time Bradford, conquerors of Arsenal. No one could begrudge Colchester their win. They played with grit and made holes in a defence in which Arsenal could find no flaw.'

George Harrison of the *News of the World* wrote 'Quite apart from the fact that they had the ball in the net five times altogether, they were speedier and more decisive in their tackling and far more business-like in their long-range game.'

Interest in U's players continued to grow with Curry and the classy Bearryman attracting bids that were quickly brushed aside. Curry had scored in every round and Bearryman's former club, Chelsea, must have regretted letting him go, especially after going out 2-0 to Manchester City. Charlton Athletic would have been fuming too over Turner's decision to throw in his lot with a non-League club and reaping such striking success.

The other fourth-round ties saw vast crowds at Goodison Park and White Hart Lane. Manchester United, playing at Goodison because Old Trafford had been bombed in the war, beat Liverpool before 74,721 people, and Spurs were 3-1 victors over West Ham in front of 71,853 people. Look at the safety-limited figures by comparison today!

The great Tom Finney scored for Preston, who beat Crewe 3-1, where there were a mere 14,000 spectators. That meant that Layer Road's 17,000-people match was not the lowest in the round of matches and that 17,000 could have been more like 25,000 if the ground had been big enough. The ticket demand was enormous and thousands were disappointed – one good reason for joining the supporters club. Membership assured one of a ticket.

Colchester had made such a name for themselves that speculation was rife when it came to the fifth round draw. Most of the big shots remained with nine representing the First Division and none of them wanted to be drawn away to the giant-killers.

As Jack Milligan of the *Daily Sketch* observed 'Everybody has been talking about Colchester being a nine-day wonder but now regard them as being one of the biggest stumbling blocks on the way to Wembley.'

The great Matt Busby, boss of favourites Manchester United, had no hesitation in declaring, 'I want to steer clear of them unless at Maine Road.'

Odds against Colchester reaching Wembley had shortened from 5000-1 to 250-1 and there were plenty of takers. Hordes of neutrals had taken them aboard as their team and were anxiously awaiting the fifth round draw. Could the non-League sensations bring it off again?

Blackpool Rock

Blackpool away – the fifth round draw brought a mixed reception. Realistically, after five successive home draws, one could not have expected to be at Layer Road again, but a trip to Manchester United or Tottenham Hotspur with a share of a potential 60,000 to 70,000 gate would have been much preferred. Just imagine little Southern Leaguers United playing before such a huge audience. It could have happened.

But Blackpool it was – the famous tangerine shirts and Stanley Matthews. One drawback was that Bloomfield Road had a capacity of only 30,000 or thereabouts. Mind you, Blackpool had a glamorous and powerful side – a sort of showbiz outfit in keeping with the entertainment playground of the North-West. One could imagine men parading outside Bloomfield Road with billboards proclaiming 'See the great Stanley Matthews magic show with full supporting star cast'. Blackpool were that type of team. Sadly though, while the Tower and golden mile are still major attractions, soccer-wise the town has drifted downhill.

In 1948, they were riding high. Apart from the peerless Matthews, there was the new quicksilver scoring sensation Stan Mortensen, classy wing half Harry Johnston, Scottish international Alec Munro and a string of other crowd-pulling names.

Mortensen was the game's first big post-war star and had an eventful war record. As a wireless operator in a Wellington bomber that was shot down, he was the only survivor, receiving severe head and back injuries. Doctors said he was lucky to be alive, but he recovered and was soon an England international.

Matthews, thirty-three, was in his prime. He had established himself with Stoke City as the wizard of dribble. Blackpool signed him in 1947 after he had spent many war years playing for them. Super-fit – he trained on Blackpool beach – he was the biggest name in the game and was in fact the pin-up hero of the Colchester dressing room.

Stanley had been top of the bill in wartime when Blackpool, with a constellation of guest players, won three cup finals with the likes of big Jock Dodds, Ronnie Dix and Eddie Burbanks. Now they were looking to conquer fresh peacetime fields.

Colchester knew they faced an enormous task. In their two previous ties, Blackpool had thrashed Leeds and Chester, scoring eight goals and conceding none. But ever the optimist, Fenton was looking on the bright side and pointed out the smallness of the Blackpool pitch. It was only slightly bigger than Layer Road and this he claimed compensated for being away.

He had the opposition watched and devised a new plan claiming to have spotted a weakness in defence and enlisting the help of former Arsenal centre half Bernard Joy in a behind-closed-doors practice game. As Fenton wanted to instruct from the sidelines, Joy played centre half and was pleased to cooperate. He was, after all, the top football writer for the *London Star* and it was a good story.

Fenton was relentless in his preparations and also sought out Maurice Reeday, a Leicester City full-back reputed to be one of the few defenders to effectively counter the Matthews magic. Reeday willingly gave him a few tips.

Joe Smith, the wily Blackpool boss of many years standing, viewed all the ballyhoo laconically, declaring his players had been instructed to regard Colchester with the same importance as if they were one of the leading First Division sides. He said 'I am too old a campaigner to be caught napping.'

As the big day drew nearer U's were adopted by hundreds of neutrals who jumped on the bandwagon and there were good luck messages from such far-flung places as Athens and the Rocky Mountains.

This was, of course, a glittering soccer era when money wasn't the king and romance reigned and it was such a lovely story when the Colchester players stayed in Matthews' seafront hotel – a temperance establishment of course. It was an unusual task for Stan to play host and then take on his guests in a momentous cup tie. Perky Len Cater, ever the comedian of the party, donned a chef's hat and was pictured with Stanley in the kitchens cooking breakfast.

Five of the players' wives stayed at a hotel two doors away, for it was a club rule they couldn't be with the team. Fred Cutting's wife said, 'We are having a great time, the boys are in fine fettle and I think they will surprise everyone again.'

The players were invited to a show starring the glamorous Pat Kirkwood. They went backstage and she autographed programmes.

When the team embarked for Lancashire they were seen off in style at a decorated Colchester station by the mayor who presented Fenton with toy black cat for good luck from his three-year-old daughter. Fenton also carried a briefcase containing his secret plan and a bag of oysters to be shared with Blackpool in a post-match celebration dinner. Again it was all first-rate publicity.

The travelling U's players were certainly a smartly dressed highly photogenic bunch – slick and confident. There was Ted himself, trilby-hatted, the boyish-faced Hillman and Kettle, dark and handsome Harry Wright and Harry Bearryman and dapper Bob Curry. Bob Allen, tall and studious, had the appearance of a college professor and Arthur Turner bore that perpetual smile. By contrast, Andy Brown would have a serious look and the chances were that joker Fred Cutting would have spent the train journey north chuckling behind the latest copy of *The Beano*! Last but by no means least, Len Cater would have been as bouncy and as full of himself as ever.

The legion of fans made the trip by other means. A few hardy types cycled north, some hired private planes and there was a special train, but the vast majority made the journey by coach, travelling through the night.

It was man-sized operation conducted in admirable fashion by supporters club social secretary, John Hammond. He had an unenviable task, for the wartime restrictions on travel and petrol still applied. There were late snags and talks with the Ministry of Transport which led to fifteen coaches being cancelled. Happily, those supporters had their money refunded and went by train.

The exodus north was simply staggering. A veritable fleet of coaches made the twelve-hour journey and the boisterous happy bands of supporters made themselves heard as they sped through the countryside. Startled late-night walkers in Midland towns and villages must have wondered what it was all about.

There were a series of adventures too. It was winter remember, and there had been snow about. One coach finished in a ditch and another had to be pushed up an icy Derbyshire slope.

It's difficult to say exactly how many people went to Blackpool – probably close to 5,000 that eventful day, Saturday 7 February 1948. Some arrived as early as 4 a.m. and the majority had arrived by dawn – Blackpool reeled under a minor invasion.

Woolworths' store was invaded and the cheerleader, the bearded Harry Fosker, and other mascots caused great amusement. There was also accordion-playing Cyril Walker leading fans in singing the song 'Up The U's'.

It turned out to be an atrociously-weathered morning with sleet and a near gale-force wind greeting the supporters thronging the streets and waiting for the pubs to open. All of Blackpool was open-mouthed in awe. The wind was so strong that one woman was blown through a plate-glass window. It really was that bad.

The weather didn't please Fenton. The last thing he wanted was a muddy pitch but that was what confronted the teams when they ran out to a frenzied roar. A crowd of 30,000 had been packed in, and the gates were closed long before kick-off time. Heartbreakingly, hundreds of

Colchester fans were locked out, having arrived at the ground late. Many had been living it up in local hostelries and had themselves to blame.

On a mud patch with rain still teeming down, U's had the worst possible start with Blackpool vitally scoring after only three minutes. It was so freakish and all started with a retaken Matthews corner after a photographer had encroached on to the pitch. I can see it now, freeze-framed in memory. Munro tamely headed goalwards, the ball assisted by the strong wind. Defenders were caught cold and a flailing Wright could only punch against the underside of the crossbar ungainly finishing up on his head with the ball in the net! If there was a soccer freak show of bizarre goals, this one, and Ray Crawford's second against Leeds scored when he was on his bottom, would surely be prime candidates.

What a different story it might have been but for this cruel stroke of luck for the underdogs. It would have been easier for the U's contingent to have seen Mortensen scoring with an explosive half-volley instead of Munro's sloppy comic cuts affair.

U's immediate response was to launch a series of attacks and we had the amazing sight of a First Division defence flat out to stop a non-League team from scoring, and on their own ground at that! Three successive corners were forced and it was the home patriots who had their hearts in their mouths. But the nearest to a goal was when Curry shot wide and Turner netted only to be given offside.

One had to admire the spirit and the calculated football that bore the Fenton trademark. Brown beat four men in an audacious run before big Jim McIntosh scored a second goal after a series of defensive mistakes, and against the run of play. It was the end. The game was already past the point of no return. Fans were silenced, wet and leaden-hearted as Blackpool took over, the combination of Matthews and Mortensen now unstoppable.

In three sensational second-half minutes, Mortensen scored twice and McIntosh got another. For his first, Morty brought the house down, beating Brown, Fenton and Bearryman in a close dribble before scoring with a shot on the run. Then he finished off a bewildering six-man move, netting from almost on the goal line and the rout was complete when McIntosh virtually walked the ball in.

At this point Matthews, who looked more a benign Sunday school-teacher than a footballer, donned his cap and gown, teasing and tormenting a now thoroughly demoralised defence. He often switched flanks and once beat five men in a mesmerising dribble. It was supreme showboating. There was a humorous incident when the perky Cater raced back to challenge the great man and put him on his back with a hefty shoulder charge. Stan is said to have remarked, 'You ought to be up front scoring goals, my lad.'

He was right of course, but this was an instinctive Cater act of retaliation. He didn't take kindly to the humiliation and Matthews certainly rubbed Colchester's noses in the dirt, or more appropriately the thick Blackpool mud, that memorable afternoon.

For the record and for those who set great store by these facts, Colchester had three corners and Blackpool nine; Colchester had eighteen goal kicks and Blackpool had twelve. Fenton's plan, part of which saw Bearryman switch from right midfield to left, had failed, but for me that sloppy first goal always rankles.

In the end, the miracle was that Colchester kept it at five. Heroic saves by Wright were a feature and he was once knocked out in saving from George Dick. He was superb.

Matthews in his book, *The Way It Was*, rather patronisingly wrote, 'To be fair Colchester kept battling to the end and did play some neat football but plan or no plan they were no match for the three M's' – Stan Mortensen, Jim McIntosh and Alec Munro.

The press were full of praise for Colchester's efforts. Ivan Sharpe, a well-known critic of the day said, 'Their movements are First Division pure and simple but they are not carried out at First Division speed.'

George Harrison of the *News of the World* wrote 'Blackpool has an M plan somewhat better than Colchester's famous F system: Matthews, Mortensen, Munro and McIntosh carved their initials deep into the hearts of Colchester supporters and ended a Cup run that had become historic. Yet it can truthfully be said that the Southern League club gave a grand show. They never stopped trying and in the first half particularly, their fighting spirit more than countered the class of their First Division opponents.'

Alan Everett, Sports Editor of the *Essex County Telegraph*, penned a superb piece under the heading 'Only England's Best Could Stop United'. Everett wrote, 'If heart and endeavour could have done it, Colchester would have won. They played themselves to a standstill and no one in

Lancashire would have begrudged them a goal.' But as one of the most knowledgeable journalists remarked, 'if Colchester could beat Blackpool on their own ground we might just as well pack up and go home because there would be no meaning left in football.' He was right, of course. We titled at the moon and if at one time it seemed within reach, it is only our own fault if we thought we could grasp it.

As broken-hearted Colchester followers began the long trek home, arriving in the early hours, the respective teams sat down to a sumptuous post-match dinner in civilised comfort, and proud skipper Bob Curry, pictured with his Blackpool counterpart Harry Johnston, was presented with the match ball. Colchester president, Alderman A.W. Piper raised a big laugh when he said, 'We are hoping to present our plan to the Government —never was a Government more in need of one.'

Fenton declared 'No excuses, none whatsoever. We have lost to a grand team. Blackpool are my new tip for Wembley.'

The other ties that February afternoon were gripping affairs. Spurs, before a 60,049 White Hart Lane crowd, beat Leicester City 5-2 and there were 67,494 at Maine Road to see Preston defeat Manchester City 1-0. Queens Park Rangers of the Third Division (South) became the new outsider hope, beating Luton 3-1 to enter the last eight.

As it turned out, Fenton was partly right with his prediction. Blackpool did go on to reach Wembley, where they lost 4-2 to Manchester United, a final reckoned to be one of the best ever. Nine of the side that licked Colchester were in action, and at one stage, Blackpool led 2-1. They were one of the top sides of the day and were back at Wembley in 1952/53 as winners, defeating Bolton Wanderers 4-3 in what was called the Matthews Final.

Colchester fans still mused over what might have happened had Matthews and company had had to cope with tight little old Layer Road. My view is that Blackpool would still have won, but certainly not by five goals. They were clearly a far better team than Huddersfield or Bradford, and Matthews and Mortensen were the leading players of the day. For all that, in hindsight I believe their players were thoroughly apprehensive about the tie. As Alan Everett in his summing up wittily wrote, 'In the first five minutes, the Blackpool men seemed to be afraid to get near a Colchester player in case he produced a secret weapon — all included in the plan — or went off with a bang.'

Colchester had to return to normality which was not easy after all the high jinks. The following week, they beat Exeter City Reserves 6-0 at Layer Road with Curry, Cutting and Turner all on the scoresheet.

Frankly though, what was left was sometimes an anti-climax and an arduous season took its toll. Some displays even brought critical comment from Alan Everett. Of a 2-0 Southern League Cup win over Chelmsford City he penned, 'The match was just about the most disappointing we have seen this season. It was miserable pointless football with more than a suggestion of bickering amongst the players and the spectators were frankly bored stiff. It was difficult to realise that this was the same Colchester team that had beaten Huddersfield and Bradford.' This was the game specially photographed for the whole ninety minutes to provide a film for instructional purposes.

Colchester of course had set high standards and, to be fair, there were some high-scoring wins, seven against Cheltenham and sixes at the expense of Gravesend and Dartford. Some players who never featured in the Cup run had a go, notably Ray Townrow, a neat and effective striker and good old Frank Rist, the former Charlton number five who frequently took over the Fenton role. He was better known as an Essex cricketer.

After the Lord Mayor's Show

The dust settled on the Blackpool experience and it's interesting to reflect again on the changing face of the game. The great invasion of the North-West did not produce one single untoward incident and crowd trouble was unheard of. Thousands of fans had to walk the streets from dawn, the weather was miserable and yet the locals seemed to treat it all as a source of amusement and amazement. It must be remembered that Blackpool drew its support from a wide radius and there was a total lack of club spirit such as existed with the U's. Blackpool Supporters Club had only 1,200 members.

A lot of pubs opened early to accommodate the wet and thirsty fans and landlords could just not believe the numbers.

The players' behaviour was equally exemplary and a code of sportsman-ship prevailed. Colchester proudly played their part and most of the players would have graced a League side. Instead, they opted for the

Southern League where the standard was high although it was not a big money game and U's wages were £7 a week full timers and £5 a week in summer. Part timers earned £3.

It was a lovely soccer age, this black and white era when players were photographed with bulky shin pads and cumbersome boots and more often than not they stood in inch-deep mud. It always amuses me too to browse through team photographs in which every player was cross-armed which was the fashion of the day.

Looking back now, Ted Fenton was the first highly acclaimed post-war manager of them all yet he might not have figured so dramatically for he at one time considered a non-playing role. Ex-Spur Albert Page and Frank Rist wore the number five shirt in the early games. U's too were the first post-war team to earn top-ranking media coverage. Their every move was spotted and reported. They had a £2 bonus for beating Huddersfield and Ted bought his wife a fur coat, his son Alan a football shirt, and his daughter some other present. The Fenton and Curry families were the most photographed, Bob with his wife, son Robert and daughter Patricia.

Bob's looks – he was of slight build and pale – belied his consummate soccer skills and it was amazing how he had recovered from his Dunkirk injuries – he had spent a year in hospital.

People who were relieved over U's ultimate defeat were the bookmakers. They would have lost a million pounds if Colchester had won. When David Cope was told of the result he said, 'Oh boy, I feel like going out and having some oysters.' His firm had been laying odds of 600-1 against Colchester and his liabilities had run into six figures.

After Blackpool, the remainder of the season saw some good results although the Southern League championship was not won then, nor in either of the following two seasons. This was really something of a mystery because U's were so talent-loaded and very much the prestige club of the non-League world, pulling in crowds home and away. Sometimes they were bigger away than at Layer Road, such was their fame and curiosity value.

Merthyr's ground record was broken when Fenton and his merry men went to Wales. Over 10,000 people packed in the antiquated ground up in the mountains, and the conditions were awful – the game being played in a blinding blizzard. When travelling across London on the underground,

Fenton was besieged by autograph hunters. When they went to works team Lovells Athletic, the Newport-based hosts had a best gate of the season with over 6,000 spectators, and Newport's High Sheriff and mayor welcomed the Colchester players. Later at Worcester, the gate was 8,600, a post-war record and in this game Ted Fenton riled the crowd with his loud verbal instructions: 'Make a record of it Ted' mouthed one wag. 'We already have!' Ted shouted back!

On occasions, the gates at Layer Road were criticised. Over the Easter period, there was a 10,440 turn-out for Guildford on the Good Friday but only 6,574 against Gravesend on the Saturday!

Then we had two games that strangely seem to have become lost in time. They were against old rivals Ipswich and Arsenal, the First Division champions, who made the splendid gesture of offering a Highbury match as a tribute for the Cup exploits. I reckon they also fancied a tilt at the team that had knocked out Bradford PA, their third-round conquerors.

The Ipswich game at Layer Road was only a friendly. It was held midweek and was taken very seriously. It was the rivals' first big meeting since 1938 and the crowd was an unbelievable 12,300. Colchester won 2-1 with goals from Fenton himself and Fred Cutting. One curious note: the light was poor and the referee played minutes short each half, but the competitive brand of football could not be disputed. As one fan said, 'If this is friendly, I'd like to see them in a cup tie.' Someone also came up with the interesting fact that Colchester had beaten teams from each division – First, Second, Third (South) and Third (North).

Arsenal on Wednesday 28 April 1948 was, for a friendly, quite extraordinary. The kick-off was 6.30 p.m. and a special train and coaches relayed well over 2,000 fans to the famous stadium. Travellers on the underground couldn't believe their eyes or ears – it was just like a cup tie.

Arsenal boss Tom Whittaker put out his first team with household names like George Male, Bryn Jones, Leslie Compton and Don Roper. The gate was a staggering 35,000, and the Highbury devotees blinked with astonishment at both the fans' antics and the quality of Colchester's football. They especially liked Kettle and one of their directors observed at one stage, 'Which is the First Division side?'

United's full giant-killing side thoroughly impressed although losing 3-0. Erstwhile Ronnie Rooke opened the scoring, Roper got the second and it was only three minutes from the end when Rooke snapped up the third.

For the record, the Arsenal were lined up thus: Swindin, Male, Scott, Jones, Compton, Forbes, Roper, Logie, Rooke, Lewis and McPherson. It was some side and the Gunners in fact finished as First Division Champions. Bryn Jones was the Welsh wizard who was the first ever £14,000 footballer and impish Jimmy Logie was one of the new breed of ballplayers and at his peak.

The season ended in a flourish and Arthur Turner collected 11 goals in the last 10 matches. Curry was also well on target and attracted a bid from Ipswich Town that was promptly rejected.

The summer saw the departure of Ted Fenton, who went back to his beloved West Ham as assistant to Charlie Paynter, whom he ultimately succeeded in 1950 to take complete charge. The move was of no great surprise, for many people felt Ted had been groomed for this job. At Upton Park he had played 176 games and was a Hammers legend. He learned much of the business at Colchester who made him a headline hero and he is close to being the club's best-ever manager.

Ted had a tremendous personality and could get the best out of players. He always had detailed reports from their previous clubs, and there is the story of how he developed Dennis Hillman one of the big hits of the cup run: although he had been a commando in the war, Hillman was shy and lacked self-confidence when he walked into Layer Road and asked for a trial. Fenton took him under his wing, encouraged him to go to dances and generally expanded his social life with startling results.

Fenton was to lead West Ham to great success including promotion to the First Division and there were several Colchester-associated players under his wing including Vic Keeble, Derek Parker, Mike Grice and John Bond who, although not a U's player, was Colchester-born. Fenton ended his managerial career with Southend United before his untimely death in a road accident.

Jimmy Allen was the new Colchester manager. Aston Villa's regular central defender in the late 1930s, he had been a sterling performer who had played for Portsmouth in the 1933/34 FA Cup final. This led to his transfer to Villa for the then headline banner fee of £10,775. He also won two England caps.

Allen was bluff but friendly and utterly uncomplicated, and players of the time talk of him endearingly as a father figure. At the outset, he still fancied playing but after a reserve game, found it too much. He was the most amiable of men and I can never recall a cross word from him – this throughout a long association with the man who was to take U's into the Football League.

When he packed up and went back to Southsea to become a publican, Jimmy often invited ex-U's players down to see him. He died aged eighty-five in 1995.

Allen's first signing was goalkeeper George Wright from Plymouth Argyle. George was to take over from the showy Harry Wright who played only five games in 1948/49. George was sound and competent and served the club magnificently. At about the same time, another of the 1948 heroes, the dour but dependable Andy Brown left. Then in the veteran stage, he linked up with Sudbury Town.

Enter on the scene at this point the enigmatical Stan Foxall. He came from West Ham where he bewitched pre-war crowds with his high skills. He was a razzle-dazzle winger as flashy off the field as on – a sharp dresser and fast talker. Foxall could operate on either flank, often popped up with spectacular goals, and on his day he was one of the most exciting players I have ever seen.

The 1948/49 campaign threw up a record that will stand for ever. Reading, then an accomplished Third Division side, were the FA Cup first-round opponents. U's cup feats were still very much remembered and it was an all-ticket match. The ceiling fixed was in fact 21,000 including ringside seats, a move objected to by Reading's boss, the famous Ted Drake. Prices remained the same as for League games and Reading took up their allocation.

The official attendance was given as 19,072 and this is recorded as Layer Road's biggest ever gate – a record that will always stand. But I question this, for it must be remembered that while 19,072 tickets were sold, it is not known how many actually attended. The day of the match, Saturday 27 November 1948, dawned with the whole area blanketed by thick fog. Trains bringing Reading fans crawled along, as did local buses and, frankly, a lot of ticket-holders outside of Colchester almost certainly did not turn up.

The kick off was an early 2 p.m. one, and the fog did lift fractionally so the referee made a start. It got worse again, and it was soon a case of players appearing and disappearing like phantoms in and out of the gloom. What happened was largely word-of-mouth communication from the field to the terraces. Bob Curry opened the scoring with a classic effort but MacPhee equalised, at which point the whole affair was rightly called off. The gate incidentally was the fourth highest in the cup that day, topping Ipswich's and Norwich's attendances.

Reading were a powerful side with an Arsenal association. Apart from manager Drake there were ex-Gunners goalkeeper George Marks and midfielder Les Henley who had been stationed locally during the war.

The big names were Maurice Edelston, one of the top inside forwards of his day and Ronnie Dix, a former Derby County and Spurs ace. Edelston was a pre-war amateur international who then turned professional. When the game was played again, it was not in midweek as generally recorded in Colchester United literature. It went ahead the following Saturday when a gate of 13,371 was recorded.

Everything turned out to be an anti-climax. From the outset, Colchester seemed strangely uninspired and there was no fog this time to hide the exceptional Edelston and Dix skills. In next to no time, two-goal Edelston, MacPhee and Dix had won it hands down, at which point Len Cater, ever a bonny fighter, shook his fist in defiance and scored twice, first with a spectacular header and then with a goal the likes of which you would never see today. He bundled Marks and ball over the line and it counted.

The local derbies with Chelmsford City were enormous crowd-pullers. City tried hard to emulate U's and had League ambitions but, more often than not, Colchester came out on top. An exception was the New Writtle Street clash which was lost by the odd goal of three. Chelmsford had brought off a coup by capturing midfielder Frank Soo, the ex-Stoke City star who had been a wartime international.

Colchester won the return 3-2 before a 14,048 gate with Keeble (2) and Curry on target, and were 3-2 winners again in a League Cup tie. Keeble invariably shone in these epic encounters and Foxall often operated on the left flank as a big favourite.

The rivalry between the Essex clubs was intense and it's incredible that twenty coaches went to Chelmsford for a reserve encounter – an Eastern Counties League Cup tie replay. Both first teams were away and the gate was 6,000-plus. Layer Road reserve gates were staggering – 5,000-plus for Chelmsford, Norwich City 'A', Spurs 'A' and Ipswich 'A'. The lowest that season was 2,561.

So that those local derbies at Layer Road could accommodate those vast crowds, ringside seating was the order of the day again. There were epic contests, the ground being full long before kick-off time.

Colchester had a poor April, winning only three of the last thirteen games. In the final match Gillingham triumphed 3-2 at Layer Road and were champions with the very good Chelmsford outfit runners-up. By a street, Colchester were the best-supported non-Leaguers and had an average gate of 9,734!

There was the unusual event of two Southern League Cup finals, and both were lost. The 1947/48 final, held over because of fixture congestion, was away to Merthyr who won 5-0, and later, Yeovil won the 1948/49 final 3-0. Season 1949/50 was the last before Football League election, packed with high excitement, goals galore and vast crowds. New faces included central defender Reg Stewart from Sheffield Wednesday and Bill Layton, an immaculate ex-Bradford and Reading midfielder and a purveyor of inch-perfect passes.

The first Chelmsford City clash saw a 16,807 New Writtle Street crowd, and a 2-2 draw. City were booming at the time and had splashed out for new big-name players – Joe Crozier, the Brentford goalkeeper, and striker Oscar Hold were both valued at £8,000, plus Cecil McCormack from Barnsley who had a £12,000 rating. That 16,807 crowd was the record for the ground alas no longer here. In 1999, it was demolished and, sadly, houses have been built on the site that had seen many a memorable game.

In the match at Layer Road, U's won 4-1 with Bob Allen (penalty) Cutting (2) and Keeble the scorers before a 14,715 attendance. Keeble was to have an astonishing season, ending with a staggering 45 goals. Curry (24) and Cutting (22) were also hitting the target and I could never fathom out why Colchester missed out on the championship. They looked certainties, but there were shock defeats to Merthyr and Gillingham and, when U's could only manage a goal-less draw at home to Barry it was lost, Merthyr taking the title on goal average.

Wright, Bearryman. Cutting and Keeble played all fifty-two games, and Foxall and Stewart missed only one. There were two opening gates of just under 10,000 and five figures were reached four times against Gillingham, Yeovil, Guildford and Tonbridge.

One major surprise was an early exit from the FA Cup to modest amateurs Wealdstone, who won by the only goal at their Lower Mead

Stadium. United fans simply could not believe that their own giant-killers were being giant-killed. The match was the first-ever Cup tie to be televised and could be put down as a complete freak result. The week before Lovells had been beaten 4-0, and the following Saturday, Kidderminster were hammered 8-0, Keeble scoring four of them.

One trophy was landed however when United took the Southern League Cup over two legs, disposing of Bath City 6-4 on aggregate. They won 3-0 at Twerton Park but, in an astonishing turn-around, lost 4-3 at Layer Road. Disappointment was expressed at the smallness of the gate, only 7,600. Today, that would be a capacity all-ticket sell-out!

Dreams Come True

Seven-Match Sensation

Colchester United waited thirteen years, including the Second World War interlude, for Football League status. It arrived in 1950 amid much celebration when the Third Divisions South and North were expanded. U's and their long-standing Southern League adversaries Gillingham were voted into the Southern Section and Shrewsbury and Scunthorpe to the Northern. For the record, Colchester polled twenty-eight votes against Gillingham's forty-four. Luckless Chelmsford City, who really fancied their chances, got only eight.

It was my pleasure to report the League baptism for the bright tabloid the *Essex County Telegraph* and the town went football mad, the U's being the sole topic of conversation. A share-raising scheme was launched and the supporters club flourished. There was a shed outside the ground for membership purposes and more than 16,000 people had enrolled at one point.

Colchester in the fifties was a most pleasing town. There were five cinemas, and the elegant High Street Cups Hotel with its imposing swing doors was in vogue, afternoon tea being the fashion. Some splendid pubs are sadly long since gone. The Fleece in Head Street, and the Essex Arms were popular meeting places for Saturday morning match discussion. The Essex Arms boasted snooker tables and was frequently used by the players.

There were no betting shops then, and if you wanted a wager, a bookie's runner like a lovable newspaper seller named Smithy was your man. He operated outside the Fleece. There was plenty of entertainment in these non-television days. The Empire was showing Johnny Weissmuller, in *Mark of the Gorilla*, to packed houses. Peter Sellers was appearing at the Ocean Theatre on Clacton Pier, the Colchester Repertory Company thrived and if one looked for a day out there were rail excursions to London for six shillings and sixpence.

There were arguments and letters to the press about so many aspects of U's elevation. Nearby residents complained at a move to build a car park in the grounds of the Cannons. And a lot of folk thought that cash raised through shares should be spent on modernising the ground.

The supporters club met the players at cricket and 300 people turned up to watch the players win. In the serious cricket world, Len Hutton hit a century for Yorkshire during the Castle Park festival week.

The supporters club ran whist drives and dances and this wonderfully laid-back age was the background for Colchester's sensational arrival. They took the football world by storm, unbeaten in their first seven matches and topped the table. It was a powerful Third Division at that time with Nottingham Forest, Crystal Palace, Millwall and local-derby rivals Ipswich Town, Norwich City and Southend United.

Boss Jimmy Allen signed well at minimal expense. Having lost the mercurial Foxall, who was banned from League football because of compensation for an injury, wingers Len Jones and Johnny Church were signed. Foxall, who linked up with Chelmsford, would undoubtedly have been a hit in the League but Jones and Church performed much better than many expected even though there were some fans who thought they were close to their sell-by date.

Jones was originally a wing half with Chelmsford and later Plymouth and Southend. He was speedy and direct and this so-amiable Yorkshire fellow was a youthful vibrant character who never seemed to age even when he quit playing and ran a popular café at the Hythe with Roy Bicknell.

Len, who was no spring chicken when Allen signed him, proved to be super-fit, and it seemed his face was forever creased in a smile. He was an expert crosser and linked effectively with Bob Curry. Reg Stewart tells of the arguments that raged between Jones and Dennis Hillman as to who was the fastest. It was finally settled between penalty area and penalty area and Len absolutely flew over the first five yards to be the undisputed winner.

On the other flank Church, dark and good-looking, proved a marauding goal getter. He had just broken into the Norwich first team when war broke out and Allen got his man in the face of strong opposition from Ipswich. Many thought Church over the top at thirty-plus but he had had a price tag of over £7,000 at one stage.

It's fascinating to look at the prices of the day. A season ticket cost six guineas and admission to the main stand was five shillings and one shilling and sixpence for the ground. When the trial match was played, the gate was 5,902, more people than Ipswich Town had for their pre-season run-out.

There was considerable publicity with the nationals and plenty of gimmicks. Jimmy Allen had a pet Scottish terrier, Andy, who used to train with the players, nosing the ball round the pitch, with the ball never more than an inch from his nose. The *Evening Standard* did a big feature on the U's with Andy in action.

The other chief U's newcomers were Johnny McKim, a dapper ball-playing inside forward whose chances at Chelsea had been strictly limited; Jimmy Elder, a tough as teak wing half from Portsmouth, and Bill Rochford, also from Portsmouth, a veteran who in fact played only one game.

McKim's football was as neat and as tidy as his appearance, and Elder was powerful and thick-thighed. He proved highly popular and had played one first-team game at Fratton Park. Many clubs were after him. For U's, he missed only one game in his first season and was the penalty taker, never failing.

The remainder of the team was made up of Reg Stewart and George Wright plus five of the old 1948 giant-killers. And the side that ran out at Priestfield Stadium for the opening game against Gillingham was Wright, Kettle, Allen, Bearryman, Stewart, Elder, Jones, Curry, Turner, McKim and Church.

The crowd, including Sir Stanley Rous, numbered 19,542 people, swelled by a large U's contingent, most of whom went to Kent by train, the excursion fare a mere eleven shillings.

A bigger crowd was expected but Gillingham would love a gate like that today. Priestfield too was a much more ramshackle arena than now.

The game ended in a dour goal-less draw, and frankly, the occasion proved too much for both sides. There was a lot of media attention too and the now defunct *Daily Sketch* had some splendid zoom camera picture coverage.

Considering Gillingham's £40,000 outlay, Colchester came out of it the better and were closest to scoring, with Church forcing Larry Gage to a desperate save. Man of the Match was unquestionably ice-cool Harry Bearryman who effected two vital goal line clearances.

Clifford Webb of the then *Daily Herald* praised Colchester's football and predicted that they would finish higher in the table than their opponents, and at the end of the season he was proved right. It was by a strange coincidence that Colchester had met and beaten the men from the Medway in their first match in the Southern League after their demotion from the Football League in 1938.

The attendances overall that opening day, Saturday 19 August 1950, were remarkable. Norwich boasted 28,269, Crystal Palace 24,811, Reading 21,793 and Bournemouth 21,430! The lowest crowd was Exeter's 10,000 against Newport, and back at Layer Road, United Reserves went down to Spurs 'A' before 4,899. All season, reserve gates were around the 3,000 mark, and this for Eastern Counties League football. Today it seems just unbelievable.

Following Gillingham, there were two more draws, a 1-1 result at Swindon and a goal-less affair at home to Bristol Rovers. So in three games, U's had scored only once and that first-ever League goal was claimed by Turner, the provider Curry, who tricked two hesitating defenders and beat a third to make the perfect opening.

The initial League game at Layer Road with Bristol Rovers grabbing a point was watched by 15,000 people and was, frankly, something of a grim unrelenting non-event. The gate was, I suppose, a little disappointing for such an historic occasion – it was 2,000 less than against Bradford in 1948. As it was, a lot of fans complained that they couldn't see and obviously there was a lot to be learned about crowd-packing.

Suddenly, the goals and wins arrived, with astonishing 4-1 victories over Swindon, Brighton and Bournemouth, plus a 3-1 triumph away to Crystal Palace.

Against Swindon, a midweek game, goalkeeper Sam Burton had a nightmare. His early misunderstanding with a defender allowed Curry to tee up Turner after only six minutes. Then, in a gripping spell just before half-time, we had a Curry lob, a Turner header and a Church side-flick all on target. Twice the hapless Burton strayed from his line and made a hash of things. Hudson got one back in the second half.

The 3-1 win at Selhurst Park was definitely the high spot. Where better for Colchester to announce themselves than in the capital? Selhurst was a major prestige stadium then and U's paraded their skills before an admiring assembly of 22,373, most of them keen to cast an inquisitive eye over the novelty new boys.

U's really turned on the style against a Palace side whose player-manager was Ronnie Rooke, the former Fulham and Arsenal goal ace. Church came into his own and laid on goals for Turner and McKim, who scored through a crowd of players. Thomas pulled one back, but Curry underlined his class and registered a third with a magnificent wind-assisted thirty-five-yard lob.

It was an extraordinary goal and guess who was the Palace keeper? None other than Dick Graham, then twenty-eight years old. Dick, who cost Palace a record fee for a goalkeeper, was caught out and grounded when Curry shot. He recovered in a vain bid to save, but finished in an ungainly heap in the back of the net with the ball. A splendid picture in the *Essex County Telegraph* recorded it so graphically. If only he had known then that Graham, twenty-one years on, would steer Colchester to the biggest cup upset of the century.

Reg Stewart reminisces about the Curry goal: 'They talk of Beckham's long-range free-kicks. People should have seen that effort of Bob's with the old styled ball at that.'

Joe Firmin wrote the *Telegraph* report and was glowing in his praise. He said that it was some performance on a pitch that was like a billiard table. At the time, there were plans to turn Selhurst into a second Wembley.

The Palace game will forever stick in my mind. It was my wedding day, a ceremony enacted over 200 miles away in Ashton, Lancashire. The match was one of only three games I missed, and I reckoned I took my solemn vows at around the time McKim scored!

The third successive win followed against Bournemouth and the 14,100 crowd was remarkable in that in this pre-floodlight age, the Thursday kick-off was 5.30 p.m. Again U's profited from a flyer, grabbing two goals in the first four minutes. With sound defence and all-out attacking wing play, the opposition was run ragged. The finishing was lethal, Turner and Curry each bagging a brace, 'Colchester Too Bracing For Bournemouth' was my *County Telegraph* match report heading.

Next we had Brighton whipped 4-1 before a 13,972 crowd, and again Curry stole the show with a connoisseur's foot in all three opening goals scored by Jones, McKim and Turner. I wrote, 'I have not seen Curry, who looks fitter and faster, playing so well. He was the leading light of an attack that is the surprise of the football world.'

Turner put McKim through for a fourth and United were pacesetting at the top with a record that read – Played 7, Won 4, Drawn 3, Goals for 15, Goals against 5. The old firm of Curry and Turner had netted 11 between them, Turner leading the way with 7. He was twenty-eight at the time and the marvellous Curry was thirty-two. They were as good as ever.

There was some controversy over that attendance figure for the Brighton match and again many fans complained that they saw little of the play with talk of the gate being rigged. Whatever, the Layer Road attendances were bigger than rivals Ipswich at this stage, but the best-supported club by far were Norwich City who more than once exceeded 30,000. Rarely did it drop below 20,000.

The crowds flocked in too at Layer Road, and those first seven games were played before 112,913 people and it was a mystery as to why the bubble burst. It did so when U's went to Bournemouth, losing 2-0, after which appropriately the first-team change had to be made, Joe Gallego coming in for the injured Church. There followed in all six successive defeats and ten games without a win, although Cutting, Keeble and John Harrison were all drafted in from time to time.

Eventually there was a recovery, the debut season ending with a respectable sixteenth placing. Jimmy Allen could sit back and reflect on a satisfactory job. He had signed nine new players at a cost of around £9,000 and it had been encouraging through the turnstiles – eleven gates of 10,000 or more, and a lowest of 6,941.

Gallego, a Spanish-born winger, Joe Lochety and John Harrison had a few games but it always surprised me why class-act Bill Layton made only eight appearances.

It was at about this time that I featured a *Telegraph* series entitled 'Home Chats With The U's'. This put the spotlight on the player's families. If any one performer epitomised these cosy stories, it was that cheery Devonian, goalkeeper George Wright, a completely uncomplicated character. He was appropriately pictured with his wife and young family enjoying a meal of bacon and eggs. It was all so unsophisticated and typical of the era.

These were days when supporters and players were much closer together. They would more than likely met on a bus or in a café and indulge in topical soccer conversation.

The lower Leagues then were of a very high quality, and each team possessed its own star name or names. Plymouth had goal man Maurice Tadman, and Southend had that Irish dazzler Jimmy McAlinden, Millwall boasted the tough Frank Neary, Notts Forest, the ultimate champions, the steely Wally Ardron, and Bristol City boasted Alex Eisentrager, a former German POW who decided to stay on in England.

It was a tough game too, and they didn't come more craggy then Neary and Ardron. Neary could play anywhere up front and could hit over corners like rockets. And what a larger than life character was Ardron, who scored both goals when Forest won 2-0 at Layer Road before a Boxing Day crowd of 12,784 people. Wally was a jack of all trades, a railway stoker, amateur boxer, swimmer and weight lifter! Reg Stewart always tells of how tough the game was, but only out in the middle. Off the park it was all handshakes, backslapping and bonhomie.

Colchester didn't have much cup luck. They still had to enter at the fourth qualifying round stage and drew Woodford at the amateurs' quaintly named Snakes Lane ground. U's had gone nine games without a win including eight defeats and some folk also wondered about a 'W' omen – there had been previous cup defeats at Wisbech and Wealdstone. But Jimmy Allen had everyone properly tuned up and Colchester romped home 7-1. In round one came a very unlucky 1-0 defeat at Bournemouth, the goal coming just four minutes from time.

It was still a soccer boom time and crowds rocketed. Even little Exeter and Torquay pulled in 8,000-odd people. The all-Bristol derby drew 31,000 and when it came to fifth- and sixth-round cup day, there were 63,000 at Newcastle and Sunderland and 50,000 at Birmingham.

Colchester didn't fare well in the series of local derbies. Ipswich, the old enemy, pulled off a double, winning a tight one 3-2 at Layer Road and cantering it 3-0 at Portman Road.

The Layer Road clash was a little unfortunate. United trailed 2-0 but came back to square with Church and Turner on target and Curry was desperately unlucky when his full-blooded drive came out off the cross-bar, Cutting failing from the rebound. It was all the more galling when, with five minutes remaining, Allenby Driver profited by a rare Curry mistake, an effort obviously intended for a centre utterly deceiving George Wright.

Driver, originally with Sheffield Wednesday, was a Norwich City discard and Man of the Match for a well-organised Ipswich side which still included veteran Mick Burns who must have been the oldest 'keeper in the entire Football League. The crowd of 14,037 people was again a little surprisingly below expectations although U's did go into the match on the back of a 7-1 mauling at Plymouth.

In the return at Portman Road over Easter, Driver, who always seemed to reserve his best for Colchester games, was again spot on with two goals. That Irish genius, Sammy McGrory, got the other. The odd feature was an out-of-the-blue first-half blizzard that swept across the ground just when a white-coated hawker was peddling ice creams! U's were well outplayed and their only chance was a return of the blizzard and a possible abandonment.

There were a staggering 21,000 spectators – a post-war record at the time – at the old Grainger Road Stadium for the first Southend game. It was an odd ground that doubled as a greyhound track, and there was so much space between spectators and the action. U's fans aplenty went seaside-bound to take in the illuminations but Southend extinguished Colchester to the tune of 4-2.

The contests against the crack Norwich side, who ultimately finished runners-up to champions Notts Forest, were close affairs and U's were a little unlucky to go down 3-2 at home. Church was injured and the ex-Canary was disappointed to miss out against his former club. Keeble took over but was out of place on the wing.

City, a slick outfit, went ahead through the gangling Roy Hollis but Cutting, another former Canary playing his first game of the season, came up with the equaliser. The first twelve minutes of the second half proved decisive when the ever-menacing John Gavin played the key role. A super winger, he was also a spring-heeled header of the ball. He made it 2-1 and after Allen had hashed a penalty – he shot yards wide – headed the conclusive third. Curry got one back and Keeble hit the bar but it was too late.

When the return game was played at Carrow Road, there was a bumper gate of 25,669 people and U's surprised everyone by drawing 1-1 – Keeble, at centre forward this time, was on target.

Colchester's new boys acquitted themselves well but two of the old guard, Harry Bearryman and Reg Stewart, were models of consistency and both played every game.

The entire season was one of ups and downs and a little piece of history was made in the Plymouth match at Home Park. The second half was broadcast by the BBC – the first time ever U's were on air. The famous Raymond Glendenning was the commentator and he made a fine gesture when booking railway sleepers on the way back for Kettle and Bearryman so that Harry could see his wife who gave birth to a daughter on the Saturday night.

As for the match, it was best forgotten, Colchester going down 7-1, for many years a record defeat. It was an odd game for at one time, it was 1-1, Curry scoring. But the second half saw a goal avalanche.

Revenge was to come at Layer Road with a 3-0 win and Keeble chalked up the club's first-ever League hat-trick. Vic was being eyed by big-club scouts and looked a born leader. Two of his goals were trademark headers, one leaving the fans wide-mouthed with astonishment. Church sent over a jet-paced low cross that Argyle 'keeper, Bill Short, was convinced was heading for touch. But from nowhere a horizontal Keeble headed home.

Colchester turned in some other good shows, especially in forcing away draws against powerful Bristol Rovers and Forest at the City Ground, when George Wright saved a penalty. Generally the away form was indifferent with only two victories, but overall a good impression was made, and U's had arrived as a League club.

The Near Miss

Fentonism, as I labelled it, returned in 1955. Benny Fenton, like elder brother Ted, came as player-manager and was to dramatically restore U's ailing fortunes. They had slipped drastically in the charts, twice finishing second from bottom, and rock bottom of the heap in 1954/55.

Jack Butler, a kindly but ailing man, finally quit with a nervous breakdown, and it needed a dynamic character like Benny to breath new life into the club. The excitement and euphoria of League football had waned more than somewhat.

Like Ted, the early career of Benny embraced West Ham, but just prior to the war, he signed for Millwall and, after hostilities, moved to Charlton Athletic where he was an inspirational captain. He took the fighting spirit with him to Colchester and was a huge success both on and off the field. A great time was the 1955/56 season, forever remembered as the near-miss season when U's finished third in Division Three (South), just a point behind promoted Ipswich and second-placed Torquay. It remains Colchester's best-ever Football League campaign.

Benny and Ted were direct opposites. Ted was tall and debonair, while Benny was stocky, excitable, quick-witted and streetwise. As a player, he was as hard as nails, a dynamic wing half who never spared himself. Invariably, he angered rival fans who, more often than not, barracked him non-stop. He often fell foul of officials and there's no doubt that in today's arenas he would have collected his full share of reds and yellows. A fitting comparison would be to say he was a cross between Vinnie Jones and Dennis Wise.

As a manager, Benny was equally as effective. With limited cash he signed shrewdly his first capture, goalkeeper Percy Ames, a Spurs reject who went on to make 423 first-team appearances.

But it was north of the Border that Fenton really succeeded. Funds were so low – the directors had to pay the summer's wages – that he raided the Scottish junior circuit with startling results. Covering 20,000 miles in six weeks, Fenton recruited John Fowler, Sammy McLeod, Bobby Hill and Chick Milligan, all for nothing. They came from romantically named far-off little clubs like Easthouses Lily, Bonnyrigg and Ardrossan. Hill, seventeen years old and frail, with choirboy looks, stayed in Benny's home until he was old enough to sign as a professional.

On later Scottish trips, Benny signed Duncan Forbes, Hamish McNeil and John Laidlaw – there was always a strong Scottish flavour about Fenton teams. They didn't all make the grade but there was high success rate overall. Benny's Scottish excursions lent themselves well to the cartoonists and this, with his beaked nose, made him a good portrait figure. Invariably, he was drawn with kilt and bagpipes!

When he came to Layer Road, Fenton was thirty-seven years old. He had been selected from forty-two applicants – there was never any shortage of managerial candidates – and he quickly devised new fitness routines. Another excellent signing, classy full-back George Fisher from Fulham, rapidly lost half a stone and regained his old Millwall form.

Benny owned an impish sense of humour. There were sometimes stories of dressing-room incidents, but the players swore by him and even today Fisher speaks in glowing terms of the man he regarded as a great manager.

I can recall one hilarious incident travelling back home from a heavy defeat. There were words between Benny and some of the directors, and next thing, Benny had told the coach driver to stop and, despite pleas to stay, disembarked. We then had the amazing sight of Benny footing it, the coach crawling alongside him for several minutes before he agreed to climb back on board and harmony was restored.

I liked Benny's wit. I used to ring him for team news and he would reel off the names ending – McLeod, McCurley, McPlant, McWright!

I must confess that we had our ups and downs. If Fenton didn't agree with my reports, he would quickly be on the phone, but any battle of words was quickly forgotten and it was as though the heated exchange never really happened.

The near-miss season began with a 3-2 home win over Southend, but there was never the hint of what was to come. Milligan and the red-haired striker Eddie Smith signed from Chelsea had good debuts. A local amateur, Les Barrell, who had been with Lexden Wanderers scored the opener but it proved to be his one and only U's goal. He played only 4 first-team games and moved to Clacton Town.

The right-wing spot was to eventually go to Tommy Williams, a chirpy flank-man who, on his day, could be brilliant. He formed a silky partnership with the skilled Hill. Williams was snapped up by Fenton from amateurs Carsharlton Athletic. Benny could certainly pick them.

The chief scorers were the stocky, consistent Kenny Plant, Kevin McCurley and the aforementioned Smith. McCurley, with his film-star looks, was originally a Jimmy Allen signing. He had his critics, but was a good striker, a dashing leader who more than once was on the point of leaving for a bigger club.

The dramatic push for the championship and promotion really got underway in December with a 5-1 hammering of Northampton Town that inspired an incredible run of twenty games without defeat. But U's were in pole position as early as September when the first of the local derbies with Ipswich came around.

Ultimate champions Ipswich were, believe it or not, fifth from bottom having won only three of their opening thirteen games. Their manager was Alf Ramsey, before he achieved immortal World Cup fame, and their revival centred around the return of ace crack-shot Ted Phillips, the big bustling Suffolk country lad who was destined for great things.

At Portman Road that day, Phillips, who had little finesse but a hammer-like shot, blasted Colchester with a brilliant hat trick in a 3-1 win and Town never looked back. The crowd was 20,413 strong, but it was more than likely that had the game been later in the season, the ground record would have been broken.

Fenton did his best with a typical sleeves-up show, taking throw-ins, free-kicks and corners and he laid on the late consolation goal for Plant. This virtuoso type of display set the pattern for the remainder of this remarkable season with Colchester turning in memorable winning displays. They led the table for so long it seemed impossible for them to fail.

Colchester were spoken of as a one-man team – Fenton, of course. But truth was the all-purpose squad were well-equipped in every area. Wingers Williams and Wright were the best in the division and goals came from all quarters. Fourteen players were in fact on the scoresheet.

The backbone of the side was defence. Percy Ames was highly reliable, and George Fisher and John Fowler brilliantly contrasting full-backs. George was immaculate in everything he did and always used the ball well. John, who had started out as a winger, was quick and liked to overlap. Chick Milligan, until he was injured, was a rock-like number five, and Bob Dale a stylish midfielder. Then of course there was a swashbuckling Fenton himself to brandish a cutlass.

Twenty players were employed, and Reg Stewart did a great job when Milligan broke his collarbone playing the last eleven games. Reg was thirty-two at the time but still a commanding figure.

The crucial centrepiece was the return clash with Ipswich Town who always posed the big threat. That Saturday 16 February 1957 was unforgettable. Town went into the match in third spot and had goal cracksman Phillips at his best – top scorer in the division with 35 goals in 29 games.

U's had won their last six on the trot and the whole business could not have been more vital and intriguing. The result was that Layer Road was jam-packed with the all-time record League gate of 18,559 people. Crowds began to assemble from an early hour, and the gates were closed with thousands outside. Chaos reigned and inside entrance and exits were blocked. In hindsight, officials must have rued not making the game all ticket.

Among those present was Football League president Arthur Oakley and had there been television it would undoubtedly have been match of the day. The atmosphere was electric and I like to picture the drama in the respective dressing rooms with that pungent smell of embrocation and air of tension. There would have been Ipswich boss Alf Ramsey, ten years later to be a World Cup hero, calmly discussing tactics. And in the other dressing room, Benny, wide-eyed and wound up with excitement, would have been stridently issuing last-minute instructions. This was the biggest East Anglian local derby of them all.

So to the game of which many spectators saw precious little. The occasion proved too much and it all ended a goal-less draw, both sides strongly claiming they should have won. Thrills and spills abounded and there were two major talking points, early on, Phillips was crocked – after a challenge from Fenton! – and then Benny himself missed a penalty.

The penalty came after twenty minutes at the Spion Kop end: Benny's shot, well placed though it was, produced a wonder save by Roy Bailey, who pushed the ball against the bar and fell on the rebound. A crush barrier went in the excitement, and some spectators were thrown on to the pitch.

Percy Ames and Bailey brought off fine saves and there were countless near-things. Wright was unquestionably the Man of the Match with his thrilling runs, and I suppose Colchester could count themselves unfortunate.

It is always argued that Fenton's spot-kick miss at the end of the day cost promotion, but it was far from a fair assessment. He was successful with four penalties and also collected 4 other goals for full measure and the main reason the big prize was missed was undoubtedly due to several other home draws that should have been wins, plus of course a disastrous run in. Injuries and illness affecting Milligan, Dale and Williams also have to be taken into consideration.

Fenton was a born leader and a wonderful inspiration in every game but especially away from home. At Bournemouth, then on a very good cup run and due to meet Manchester United, Benny silenced the 21,239 crowd with a late volleyed equaliser. He had been booed every time he had the ball, pelted with orange peel and spoken to by the referee. But he was impervious to it all and had the last laugh, something which was so often the case.

That gate was the best of the season and Fenton came out tops against a similarly styled adversary striker, Ollie Norris, who had a reputation for gamesmanship. He had a fearsome war-cry, yelling 'Ollie, Ollie, Ollie' as he charged for goal!

In the next game, close rivals Torquay were beaten at Layer Road before a 12,555 crowd – the crew-cut Bobby Hill was the wizard and matchwinner, and U's then had a four-point lead at the top and in those days it was two points for a win.

Promotion was within touching distance but Easter as so often proved the crunch. It was three games in four days then and a test of stamina and fraying nerves. On Good Friday – gate 12,770 – Walsall were beaten 2-1 at Layer Road. This time, Fenton scored from the spot and wonderboy Hill, who looked a world-beater, hit the winner.

Bobby was one of Benny's best-ever Scottish captures, a crew-cut boyish-faced genius who should by all rights have risen to the very top, but he stuck to Colchester and ultimately responded to another calling and remains today a Jehovah's Witness.

For the remainder of that hectic holiday, it sensationally all fell apart at the seams with two defeats. At a dust bowl of a Den it was Millwall – one of Benny's first loves – dishing out a 3-1 mauling and at Fellows Park Walsall turned the tables from Friday, winning 2-1.

The Easter tragedy was crucially decisive. The Millwall game, played in uncharacteristic heat, saw the end of the twenty-match run without defeat. A rather sloppy goal by John Shepherd in nine minutes got U's off on the wrong foot but Ken Plant levelled after a solo run by Peter Wright. For a while, U's were on top until two second-half goals by John Summersby killed them off.

On Monday it began brightly with Eddie Smith opening the scoring, but Walsall, with four reserves, played well above themselves. The whole business was now on a knife edge. With two games left, Colchester and

Ipswich were joint top, Town owning the better goal average. But U's penultimate fixture was away to second from bottom Swindon and plenty of confidence remained.

Fenton and his troops embarked to Wiltshire with high hopes, but what transpired at the County Ground that fateful April afternoon was a sheer nightmare. U's were set to face a near gale and as a result an inspired Swindon were three up at the end of twenty-four minutes and it was game, set and match.

I have seldom seen a Colchester side so dispirited and demoralised. Ames was handicapped by injury and although a desperate Fenton played himself into the ground nothing went right. Swindon even missed a penalty before adding a fourth. Plant's reply counted for nothing and it was a gloomy trip back home when everyone had hoped to be celebrating with champagne.

Fenton had an ankle injury and had to sit out the final fixture at home to Watford and reliable Bert Hill was an able deputy. The gate was 9,226 and I often ponder as to what it would have been had U's won at Swindon. The 19,000 ground record might have been under threat. As it was Colchester won 2-0 and a sliver of hope remained. Ipswich and Torquay had to fail in their away games the following day.

It was not to be. Ipswich won 2-0 at Southampton to finish top on goal average, and Torquay drew at Crystal Palace. The top duo had 59 points each and Colchester 58. Fourth-placed Southampton were 6 points in arrears.

The anti-climax for what was arguably Colchester's best-ever squad caused heartbreak. They were unbeaten at home and were fantastically supported.

Twenty players were used and had they been handing out soccer Oscars for best-supporting player, it would have been between Bert Hill and Eddie Smith. Bert was as cockney as the Elephant and Castle, a bustling midfielder who never shirked a tackle and relished a full-blooded contest as his catalogue of knocks and injuries testified – he collected black eyes by the score. The red-haired Smith was not a regular but scored vital goals. He and Hill were great buddies having signed for Chelsea on the same day.

It was, all in all, a historic turning-point season. Ipswich, after the strongest challenge ever from their rivals went on to achieve greatness. Who knows how events would have gone had the roles been reversed? As it was U's were so near and yet so far and decades later we are still awaiting a similar momentous campaign.

Arsenal Thrills

Benny Fenton deliberated at length over his playing career after the excitements of 1956/57. In the end, he decided to keep going and played twenty-three more games before finally calling it a day, his concluding match against Southampton.

Benny was forty and really something of a marvel. Super-fit, he was well summed up by the late Doug Ibbotson of the then *News Chronicle*, who wrote after a 2-1 win at Gillingham, 'Fenton virtually won the game by will power. There is no more inspiring sight in soccer than Fenton moving at speed. The jaw is set, the neck thrust forward, legs pounding like flails.'

At the time, Benny was one of the most-discussed managers in the country and Colchester had to resist a move from his former club Charlton who wanted him to take over from the ageing Jimmy Seed. There was a lot of nonsensical talk too that United had not really wanted promotion, as they were financially ill-equipped for higher-grade football.

In point of fact, they had drawn up plans for a new stand and looked to enlarge the ground to accommodate 25,000 people, also increasing the playing staff to twenty-five. Any idea that promotion was not wanted was surely completely dismissed by Fenton's superhuman efforts. He literally played himself into the ground.

Needless to say, the plans were all scrapped when promotion was missed. But the new season became crucial as it decided who played in a new Third Division, the Southern and Northern sections being discarded. It was a move that caused some controversy as it would be mean far more travelling.

The top twelve teams qualified and, in the end, U's just made it by beating Southampton 4-2 and on the scoresheet was Russell Blake, a winger who Fenton had drafted in earlier in the season. Blake was a part-timer, a local accountancy clerk who possessed an electric burst of speed and was a superb crosser of a ball. Subsequently, he came into his own in a big way.

The season was packed with incident and, at long last, the long unbeaten home run was ended. It lasted an incredible twenty-seven games, finally broken by Reading who pirated a 3-1 win. Fenton decided to strengthen the team, and for biggish fees, signed striker Neil Langman, a giant of a man, from Plymouth Argyle and lanky Liverpool forward John Evans, a player whom Fenton knew well from his Charlton days.

The pair were recruited in the wake of a disastrous early 1-0 FA Cup exit to unfancied non-Leaguers Wisbech Town, who delivered a surprise Fenland Park knock-out blow, the winner coming from ex-Wolves veteran Jesse Pye.

Fenton didn't play in this one and I shudder to think of what the dressing room atmosphere was like afterwards. Benny, in many games especially away from home, was still public enemy number one with many fans and, in one barnstorming local derby against Norwich at Carrow Road, was booed from start to finish.

He managed 3 goals in this, his last campaign. New boy Langman did well with 8 but the top scorer by far was trusty, dependable Kenny Plant with a bag of 19 goals.

The cup flop was a major disappointment and the dizzy exploits of Ted Fenton's 1948 storm troopers were becoming a far-off memory. But everything changed in 1958/59 with a run that ended in the glamour tie every small club dreams about: Arsenal at home.

Events began with a cosy 2-0 win over Southern League Bath City whose player-manager was none other than Stan Mortensen, portlier and slower since the 1948 excitement. Langman and Plant did the necessary.

Then came a scare against another Southern League club in Yeovil, themselves famed cup fighters who in 1949 sensationally knocked out Sunderland. At Layer Road, U's were favourites, but were held to a 1-1 draw. Plant scored but it was very much a below-par show and nobody relished the prospect of playing Yeovil on their infamous slope, the graveyard of so many. Benny must have read the riot act; Colchester, with Tommy Williams taking over from Blake, gave a sparkling display, winning 7-1.

They ran the famous green shirts ragged on a skidding top, and wingers Williams and Wright were devastating. Langman, back in his own neck of the woods, scored four, diminutive Sammy McLeod hit a brace and Williams got the other. It was rare for little Sammy to score as he was invariably a goal maker. He cost just £10 and might have been sold five times over as clubs were constantly eyeing him. Later that season, he seemed set for Chelsea for £15,000, a big fee in those days. But it fell through and Sammy saw his career out at Colchester, emigrating to Australia where he was tragically killed in a road accident.

In the third round, luck held good with another home draw against Chesterfield and the legendary Gordon Banks. This game was something of a lottery on an ice-bound pitch and Chesterfield had the better of the first half. But U's, with Blake back for Williams, rallied, Johnny-on-the-spot Evans and Langman steering them through. Maybe the borrowed continental reserve strip of West Ham helped.

Excitement was at fever pitch when mighty Arsenal were drawn – it was always a Monday morning radio business then. The Gunners, managed by George Swindin, sat proudly at the top of the First Division and were a class act: whenever was it not the case with an Arsenal team?

They had six internationals: goalkeeper Jack Kelsey, the colourful Tommy Docherty, Dave Bowen, Danny Clapton, Dave Herd, Jackie Henderson and Bill Dodgin. Kelsey and Bowen had both featured in the World Cup.

Vic Groves, who had once starred for Leyton Orient in a horrendous Colchester defeat, was another star name and striker Len Julians, also ex-Orient, was a player Fenton had tried to sign earlier in the season.

Swindin's first reaction was, 'Well, well, away again, I don't like the draw at all. From what I hear, we are facing a pretty useful side.' He must have had in mind Arsenal's shock defeat to Northampton the previous season.

The week before the match Arsenal whacked Everton, and U's game at Rochdale was called off. Meanwhile, Benny and secretary Claude Orrin had the unenviable task of dealing with ticket demands. Claude was meticulous, dapper and, all in all, highly efficient – the perfect secretary who served the club magnificently for many years.

Benny's phone threatened to jump off the desk as the applications poured in for this was a game everyone wanted to see. The crowd limit was 16,000 – 15,000 in the ground at three shillings and 1,000 for the stand prices for which were seven shillings and sixpence and six shillings.

The 16,000 ceiling met with all-round approval and Fenton said, 'This is a great day for the club. We don't want anything to go wrong and we want everyone to see in comfort'. He added that packing in, say, 19,000 people would cause discomfort and fans sprinkled around the touchlines would clearly and unfairly affect Arsenal.

The Saturday prior to the big match, 4,000 tickets went on sale and there were amazing scenes. The sale was not due until 1.30 p.m. but it started at 7 a.m. with queues snaked back to the Drury Hotel. In next to no time, all tickets had gone. About 1,500 people were turned away empty handed.

As the match drew nearer, there was a lot of the old 1948 ballyhoo and Bernard Joy, now writing for the *Evening Standard*, took part in a behind-closed-doors practice affair which meant that history repeated itself. Joy, the former Arsenal centre half, had done the same in 1948. He predicted that Langman would be the danger man.

There were shades of 1948 again when Ted Fenton sent a good luck telegram and superstitious Benny told skipper George Fisher to carry it in his shorts during the game. Another story for the mystical Meg brigade involved the latest mascot, Whisky the terrier dog, whose owner, ex-Welsh miner Taffy Richards, took him to nearly every away ground. The lovable little dog in his blue and white coat, when questioned as to who would win, barked twice!

John Evans was ordered by Fenton to turn back the pages of his scrap-book. Hidden away was the report of a smash-hit Charlton win at Highbury in which Evans scored twice. Fenton recalled the game and said, 'I was in the same side and John had a blinder. In fact I can never remember him having a bad game against Arsenal. He seems to have an Indian sign on them.'

So to the game, Saturday 24 January 1959, another of those red-letter Layer Road days forever recalled. It was an epic of high-quality football and there was never a bad foul. U's unquestionably played First Division football and took the game to their famous opponents, McLeod spinning his magic. Blake, who kept the right-wing spot, and Wright always menaced on the wings and at the back, man to man marking was tight and effective with target man Groves most subdued.

Thrills abounded at both ends and Kelsey brought off a great save from Wright, while Percy Ames tipped over a scorcher from Herd – the longer this enthralling contest lasted, the more a goal seemed unlikely, especially when a rocket shot from Danny Clapton rebounded off the inside of a post into Ames arms. U's other big let off was when Derek Parker woofed off the line another Clapton effort.

Finally, in the 75th minute the deadlock was broken. John Fowler, who had been magnificent, made a rare error and slipped, Clapton beating him on the inside. A square pass and Groves made no mistake. A minute later Gerry Ward's chipped cross was headed in by the jubilant Groves and it was as good as over and certainly would have been but for an Ames wonder save to deny Jackie Henderson.

What followed was not for the weak of heart. On 80 minutes, never-say-die Langman pounded down the middle like a dreadnought under full stream, brushing past four red shirts before hammering the ball home and two minutes later the whole ground erupted. The silky McLeod slipped a pass to Wright whose low cross Evans turned over the line at close range and U's had come back from the dead.

It's strange how, yet again, a sheer piece of soccer drama had been enacted at what was always termed the favourite Layer Road goal end, and there was all but the sensation of a Colchester win as Arsenal, reeling like a punch-drunk boxer on the ropes, somehow survived the final pulsating minutes. There was no stoppage time those days. Had there been, I'm utterly convinced Colchester would have triumphed.

How old man Fenton would certainly have relished being out there for the rip-roaring finale. Instead he was crouched on the touchline, a frenzied figure urging his players on for one last desperate effort. He switched from a pipe to cigarettes and hours later was still hoarse. He could only croak, 'We were magnificent. I wish all Britain could have seen us'. Swindin moaned, 'Even if we had been four or five up there is no way a defence should fool around as we did.' But he offered his congratulations.

It was certainly Langman's top moment. The 14-stone-plus Devonian was deceptively lumbering. He had tapering legs which ensured perfect balance, was great in the air but also equally effective with surprisingly good footwork. Although a giant of a player, he was mild of manner and highly protective of the then young Peter Wright. I always remember him too, cradling little Sammy McLeod in his arms back to the centre spot after a goal had been scored.

Colchester in hindsight performed superbly. There was a magical fifty-yard run by Wright past four men ending at the by-line and a pass that Evans turned over the bar. Testimony to U's command also were their eight corners to Arsenal's five.

It was a brilliant all-round display and mention should be made of versatile Derek Parker, that very dependable wing half. He was a

Rowhedge lad who slipped the local net when a youngster, going to West
Ham where he starred successfully. Married to a local girl, he returned
home and played 137 games in U's colours.

There were a host of personalities present – Arsenal were as always a
show-biz type of club. There were John Arlott, Pete Murray, Jack Train and
fervent Gunners fan and comedian Ted Ray. Also present were over 100
photographers and pressmen, some of whom were caught on the hop.
Harold Palmer of the *Evening Standard* was one of them. He wrote, 'Two
goals in two minutes finished Colchester off', and you had to look in the
Stop Press for the Colchester goals!

Ian Woolridge, arguably today's number one sport columnist, was then
writing for the *News Chronicle*. He waxed enthusiastically, 'At 4.13 p.m.
Arsenal were leading 2-0 and I have yet to meet the man who could
truthfully say he didn't consider it was curtains for Colchester.' He added,
'Can they complete the sensation at Highbury after tearing up one obitu-
ary notice when they came back from the dead? I refuse to write them
off.'

For the Wednesday night replay, hysteria reigned. It is difficult to convey
the fervour and there was mass exodus to London with factories and
shops closing early. The estimate was that 10,000 people went to
Highbury, most via seventy coaches and four special trains. Hundreds
journeyed by car but the overall result was absolute anti-climax. Arsenal
put Saturday well behind them and won 4-0.

What made it worse was the cold foggy night – it was difficult to follow
the play – and the fact that the gates were closed thirty minutes before
kick off with many Colchester supporters locked out. It was completely
chaotic with 62,365 fans inside, mounted police in action and a breakdown on the underground for good measure.

Out on the icy treacherous pitch, events were equally crazy. Arsenal,
hell bent on redemption, played like world-beaters and were home and
dry at before Kelsey had to make a save. It was utterly one-sided and
heartbreaking for the U's patriots. Amazing statistics were revealed –
Arsenal having thirty-nine goal attempts before Colchester's first shot in
the 72nd minute and then Evans shot straight at Kelsey.

The Arsenal keeper, it was also recorded, didn't have to take a single
goal kick and as John Camkin of the *News Chronicle* wrote, 'This is, I
imagine, unique in first-class football. I cannot recall a match so

completely one-sided, but Colchester at least went out with dignity, cash – around £3000 – and courage.'

The 62,365 crowd is still the biggest ever for a Colchester game, a record that will surely never be beaten and it has to be said U's took their defeat sportingly, penalised only three times – a remarkable feat in such a one-sided affair.

The other incredible fact was that there was only a goal in it until the 52nd minute thanks largely to the brilliance of Ames. The first goal on eighteen minutes was the result of a defensive error, following non-stop pressure. Milligan headed away a cross instead of leaving it for Ames, and Len Julians, who had come in for the injured Jimmy Bloomfield, teed up Herd for an easy kill.

It was seven minutes into the second half before another defensive slip let in Herd and as the fog began to thicken, only an occasional burst by Wright raised U's hopes. It was all over as Bowen, brilliant throughout, laid on a goal for Julians and Dennis Evans despatched a penalty after the gallant Ames had hauled down Groves.

In the press room afterwards, a happy Swindin told of his players wearing crêpe-soled boots with no studs which they had used in training. They turned out to be match-winners on the icy surface.

The *Colchester Express* turned over its entire front page to the replay with a mammoth heading that read 'We're Out' alongside another of those graphic Des Blake photographs illustrating a typical Ames save.

So U's returned to League action and at Layer Road, where they had been so close to history the week before, Doncaster Rovers were beaten 1-0. Disgust was expressed at the gate – a mere 8,658!

And what of Arsenal? In the next round they were knocked out by Sheffield United and the cup was surprisingly won by Nottingham Forest who beat Luton 2-1 in a low-key final.

Colchester, who had been a sound fancy for promotion, finished in seventh spot, but gates declined and there were two very lean Fenton seasons with relegation in 1960/61, the more surprising as Newcastle were unloaded in a Football League Cup tie.

There was a rapid promotional return in 1961/62, a campaign crammed full of goals with Bobby Hunt and Martyn King leading the way. Hunt was absolutely fabulous and ended up with 39 – still the most in a season. Among the many comprehensive wins was the record busting

9-1 walloping of Bradford City, and it was a pity that some of the shine was taken off the achievements by Ipswich Town's astonishing feat of taking the First Division championship.

Finally in November 1963, Fenton left to take over Leyton Orient. Bigger clubs had been hankering after him, but I always believe Benny was in two minds and he had a very soft spot for Colchester who gave him a fond farewell with a 1-0 FA Cup win at Brighton thanks to a Hunt goal.

As it turned out Fenton did not stay long at Brisbane Road, as he was sacked with two years of his three-year contract left. At Layer Road he had reigned supreme for more than eight years, the longest-ever serving manager. He was a legend especially for his playing performances – 106 memorable games. He finally passed away aged eighty-two.

The Man From Bogotá

For Fenton's successor, the Colchester board chose Neil Franklin from a shortlist of four. Franklin was reckoned to be England's most classic centre half ever who had created a storm in 1950 when he walked out of Stoke City to try his luck in Bogotá for big money. He was the country's first-ever soccer rebel. He had played forty successive games for England and they never picked him again. Subsequently Franklin joined Hull City for £20,000 and then had a succession of minor clubs including Crewe, Stockport, Maccesfield and Wellington. The South American experience was something of a misadventure and left him thoroughly disenchanted. He came back with nothing in fact.

Franklin went abroad again to coach in Cyprus from where he came to Layer Road paying his own air fare, about £90, such was his desire to return. Colchester treated him well with a good salary, a Ford Corsair car and a club house for him and his attractive wife, Vera. And they reimbursed that air fare.

There were several well-known names on the shortlist, and frankly, others had better managerial experience than Franklin, but the Colchester directors were impressed with his name and accomplishments. Franklin is beautifully summed up by Stanley Matthews in his autobiography. Stan said, 'He won everything in the air and tackled with superb timing. And when the ball was at his feet, he possessed the nous to pass it with all the guile and intelligence of the most cerebral of inside forwards.'

He went on, 'When it came to heading he was as dominant in the air as a Spitfire. Many a time was the game played in pelting rain and on a gluepot of a pitch when all the Stoke players would leave the field covered in mud except Neil whose shirt and shorts would be just specked with splashes. The only sign he had been in the thick of it would be the brown circle of mud hammered on to his forehead.'

The first thing you noticed about Franklin was his looks. Debonair and slim, he appeared years younger than forty-one, a veritable ageless Peter Pan. There was never a hint of grey in his dark hair and the only facial lines to be seen were laughter lines.

As he said at the time, 'I have been lucky especially when I see how some people in football seem to have aged. But then I have never been a worrier and take life as it comes. I've made mistakes – who hasn't? – and it was a bit stupid of me to go to Bogotá like that. But I'm not bitter. Why should I be? I like football and I'm doing the thing I like. It's a wonderful game that keeps me young.'

As when he dominated the playing scene, immaculate in everything he did, Franklin was always calm and unruffled. Only once did I remember him being agitated. It was a promotion year, and United had lost their last game 2-1 at Newport. Then Franklin sat with me for a good ten minutes in the Somerton Park press box awaiting a phone call with the results of other matches that had kicked off later. Happily they were the right ones and United went up by 0.2 of a goal. Luton were the threat and were leading, but a late goal made it 1-1 and Franklin and the small band of travelling fans lived it up.

Great a player as Franklin had been, he was never popular with the fans or many of the players. He sold local idol Bobby Hunt to Northampton Town for £20,000, which many thought was a giveaway price, and at the same time, he acquired a string of players who were mediocre, to put it mildly. Gary Salisbury, Pat Connolly and Ray Price readily spring to mind.

But there were some good signings: Derek Trevis from Aston Villa, Brian Hall from Mansfield, Terry Price for a bargain £3,000 from Orient, and Reg Stratton, an elegant striker who scored 60 goals in three seasons.

Not everyone agreed with Franklin when he brought off a deal with Luton exchanging great favourite Billy Stark for ex-Ipswich crack-shot

Ted Phillips, who scored a debut hat-trick – all headers – against Barnsley, but left at the end of the season after scoring 13 goals in 34 games. It was strange that he missed three penalties, something that never occurred when he was at Portman Road. He was reckoned to be the hardest shot in the game.

That Philips debut was remarkable. He was thirty-two years old at the time and had been in dispute with Luton. He only started training five days before his first Colchester match, yet within fifty minutes, he had scored three goals. Phillips put at least 1,000 on the gate, which was 5,082, and the fans loved him. This was his answer to accusations that he was a forgotten has-been. He was a big personality and no mean cricketer – at times, a devastating fast bowler for Colchester and East Essex.

The *Colchester Express* made hay of his debut: 'Ted packs 'em and heads 'em in' was my match report heading and that ace cameraman Des Blake brilliantly captured all three goals.

It was a time when U's were looking for a boost and I offered a guinea weekly for readers for the best and most feasible suggestion to raise their spirits. I suggested maybe a military band at half-time, a pop group before the match and, ludicrous as it seems now, open-air wrestling prior to kick-off. There was the introduction of a licensed bar on the popular side and a new look programme. But nothing else happened, not even the hoped-for promotion.

Talking of Phillips again, it was delightful to see him recently on a splendid TV programme on Sir Alf Ramsey. Ted in his seventies looked much the same hale and hearty and as rural Suffolk as you could get. He paid an eloquent tribute to Sir Alf with whom he had been closely associated.

Franklin's reign proved one of constant ups and downs. His first full season ended in relegation to the Fourth Division and, although there was a return at the first attempt, they never made any real impact. By the time he departed, U's were down once more.

Franklin was low in the popularity stakes when he sold Martyn King to Wrexham for modest cash plus an exchange for midfielder Tec Jones who came with a big reputation but frankly turned out to be a flop.

Most supporters felt that King was undersold. He certainly seemed set for a bigger stage and there is little doubt that had he been around today he would be a Premiership leading light. He had been a Fenton signing from the famous amateur club Pegasus, and Benny persuaded him to turn professional with immediate success. He remains Colchester's record top scorer – 132 in 227 games.

King specialised in hat-tricks and there was one that was specially spectacular in a local derby against Norwich, the first goal coming in twenty-five seconds. But a lot of fans objected to what often appeared to be his shrug-of-the-shoulder indifference. It was in fact just a quirk of character.

He too thought he was misunderstood. I wrote glowingly of him on one occasion, calling him 'mean, moody and magnificent'. Martyn took exception although it was all meant as a high compliment.

It was not surprising that King and Franklin never really saw eye to eye. King once said, 'To put it mildly I did not get on very well with him. You might call it a clash of personalities. I realise I was not the easiest of blokes to get on with but I certainly wasn't the only one to be put out by Mr Franklin.'

Upon leaving, King's career plummeted and he wound up with Welsh non-League club Porthmadog, finally calling it a day with ligament trouble.

Personally, I found Franklin cooperative and with a charming personality. Maybe he was not quite ruthless enough as a manager and was often criticised. But in 1967/68, he did remarkably well to get United through a particularly tricky FA Cup tie against Chelmsford City to set up a glamorous money-spinner against West Bromwich Albion.

Southern League Chelmsford had always envied Colchester's League status, and were a powerful outfit at the time, having disposed of Oxford United in the previous round after two replays. They had feared strikers in Tony Butcher and Bill Cassidy, had home advantage and, having beaten Colchester in an Essex Professional Cup tie, fancied their chances of a prestige win in downing the 'old enemy'. They were certainly favourites.

Colchester went into the game with a thoroughly indifferent run of results. But for all the apprehension before a packed New Writtle Street crowd of 16,400, they rose to the occasion magnificently winning 2-0. It was a superb professional display built on the defensive rocks of Derek Trevis and craggy Duncan Forbes, a physically intimidating duo if ever there was. Butcher and Cassidy were reduced to mere mortals and City was run ragged by wingers Terry Price and Johnny Martin. Tommy McKechnie volleyed a fine goal and it was all Colchester until Stratton scored in the last minute.

1 *Huddersfield Town, 1948 – the two teams.*

2 *Bradford, 1948. The teams line up before a packed Spion Kop end.*

3 Left *Len Cater, a giant-killer in his prime.*

4 Below *Goalkeeper, handsome Harry Wright.*

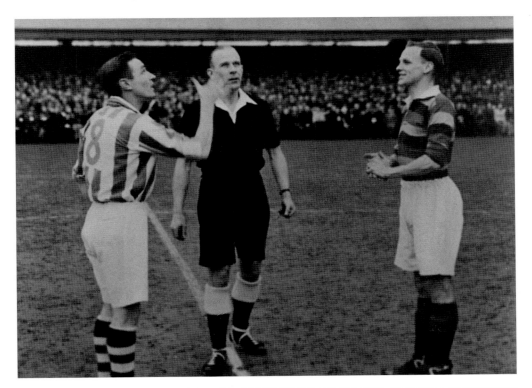

5 Top *Pre-Bradford, the toss-up. Bob Curry and Bradford skipper Bill Greenwood.*

6 Bottom *Post-Bradford, Curry and Greenwood in mufti enjoying a cuppa.*

7 *The first goal v. Bradford – a Bob Curry header.*

8 *Second half v. Bradford. Fred Cutting tests Chick Farr. Note the fans on the stand roof and the ringside seats.*

9 Above *The ever-smiling Arthur Turner.*

10 Left *Ace winger Dennis Hillman.*

11 Left *Pre-Blackpool, 1948. The great Stan Matthews entertains the U's in his seafront hotel – and chef Len Cater lends a hand.*

12 Below *The umbrella man mascot Harry Fosker leads out the team at Bloomfield Road.*

13 Opposite *The irrepressible Digger Kettle.*

14 *Historic team line-up in the game lost in time, Arsenal v. U's before their friendly at Highbury in 1948 which attracted a 35,000 crowd.*

15 *High-priced collectors items – big-match programmes from 1948.*

16 *Bob Curry in later years with the Blackpool match ball.*

17 Above *Brian Hall in typical action.*

18 Left *Benny Fenton was a cartoonist's dream. A fascinating cover of a 1960s supporters club handbook.*

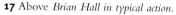

Colchester United SUPPORTERS CLUB ANNUAL 1960 – 1961 PRICE SAX PENCE

19 *Scoring sensation: Bobby Hunt in his prime.*

20 Above *Merseyside-bound. Happy fans on the way to Goodison.*

21 Below *An extraordinary picture of the Everton cup tie – a watching Graham Smith in front of the packed main stand – did we really lose 4-0!*

22 Above *Man of the Match Mick Mahon gets in his cross in the Watney Cup final.*

23 Above *Watney Cup winner – Phil Bloss, cool, calm and collected, dispatches the final penalty!*

24 Below *Still rolling out the barrel. Dick Graham and the lads on a town victory procession.*

25 *Jubilant skipper Bobby Cram held aloft with the handsome trophy.*

The gate was actually just 400 short of the ground record and, as it turned out, exceeded the Layer Road attendance for the fourth round Albion tie that followed. It all underlined yet again the mystery of why Chelmsford never gained League membership. Year after year they were the nearly men – the likes of Hereford, Wimbledon and Oxford sneaking in. Constant financial upheavals culminated in them quitting New Writtle Street and, sadly, the stadium is no more and they have been ground-sharing with Billericay.

Franklin was in pain through a slipped disc, but he was overwhelmed by Chelmsford's sportsmanship and hospitality. City supplied the champagne to celebrate and he said, 'In my twenty-eight years in professional football, I have never come across such generous opponents in defeat. My players and I were highly impressed with the sporting manner in which City took their disappointment.' City were indeed a lovely club at all times.

The fourth-round clash with WBA on Saturday 27 January 1968 saw Layer Road buzzing again with a big crowd – the gate was 15,981 – and the Throstles were mighty lucky to escape with a replay.

It was Franklin's shining hour and Reg Stratton proved a revelation. The former amateur international put U's ahead and only the underside of the crossbar denied him a second.

The move that led to this turning point incident is worthy of detailed description. There was a sizzling move between Johnny Martin and Tommy McKechnie who pulled the ball back from the byline over John Osborne's head at speed, Stratton came crashing in and his header looked a goal all the way until the ball rocketed out off the woodwork. It was breathtaking.

Stratton had given Franklin orders to 'get at them' and this was unquestionably his best ever U's game. Albion were clearly rattled, and owed everything to a controversial spot kick.

Colchester looked the First Division side but then Forbes was adjudged to have brought down the legendary Jeff Astle and it was a hotly disputed penalty that Tony Brown gratefully despatched. Former Arsenal star Joe Hulme, writing for the *Sunday People*, reckoned the decision one of the harshest he had seen. He added, 'Colchester gave them one hell of a fight and the final whistle must have been sweet music to Albion.'

This was certainly the case in a drama-packed finish. With seconds left on the clock, John Mansfield netted after Trevis had hit the bar. But referee

Alan Jones decreed that Stratton had handled in the build-up play. Stratton insisted he had chested the ball down, but the unruffled Franklin said, 'The referee was right on the spot. I can't argue with him.'

The match produced plenty of publicity and nippy little Price was in the news. His father had a popular Colchester fish shop and Terry was pictured outside with a banner proclaiming, 'Special this week WBA with chips!' Terry was also pictured with his wife-to-be, seventeen-year-old Lynn Brackwell from Leyton.

But the replay at the Hawthorns was sheer anti-climax. Not for the first time in away cup ties, Colchester collapsed like a pack of cards. Roared on by a 40,008 crowd, Albion were home and dry after half an hour, three goals up with John Kaye and Astle (2) on target. It was one-way traffic and Clive Clark added a fourth late on. Scottish star Bobby Hope was the Man of the Match and plotted three of the goals.

Albion had Dick Sheppard in goal for the jittery Osborne and made no mistakes this time, but U's had their moments, and forced the first corner when Sheppard tipped away a Price free-kick. Largely, however, it was 'keeper Ernie Adams who featured with some brilliant saves.

Ernie, who came from Arsenal, is a little-remembered player who made only 48 appearances before leaving for Crewe.

Albion never looked back and went onto Wembley to lift the trophy, beating Leeds United with an extra-time goal by Astle who scored in every round. Albion also equalled Newcastle's record of appearing in ten finals but always reckoned their luckiest moments were at Layer Road.

It was a good Colchester team but for all their cup exploits they were relegated. The two top players were, without doubt, Trevis and Forbes. The former Villa man was Player of the Year and eventually moved to Walsall. After that, he emigrated to America where he became a successful businessman.

Forbes, a true Scot with an accent to match, was a veritable rock. The most amiable of fellows, he was a stalwart defender for six seasons and finished his career on a high plane with Norwich City for whom he later scouted. And what of Mansfield, so close to being the hero at Layer Road? He was a local lad whose promise was never fulfilled. He made only 42 appearances and went non-League with Brentwood.

So United were relegated. After West Brom, they lost three on the trot and won only one of the last twenty games, ending with a horrendous

5-1 home defeat to Peterborough, condemning them to the Fourth Division – all over again. The gate for that match slumped to 2,483, a new all time low.

Inevitably, Franklin was dismissed. The board reckoned that there had been little cooperation between manager and players and a lack of method and leadership.

Franklin said, 'Running a club on a shoestring budget leaves little scope and if things go wrong it is the manager who has to go.' Franklin in fact drifted out of football, took over a pub in Lancashire, and died aged seventy-four in 1996. His ventures into managership unfortunately never matched his immaculate playing career.

King Dick Rules

Leeds and all that

Dick Graham, the next choice for the hot seat, arrived in 1968. There were no fanfares. They came later. The salary was £2,500 a year plus a car. Graham was forty-eight and a former Northampton Town and Crystal Palace goalkeeper and, while there was nothing extraordinary about his playing career, he turned out to be one of the most discussed managers of his day.

Graham made his mark taking Crystal Palace to promotion and he became a folk hero at Selhurst. Later he coached West Bromwich Albion and managed Leyton Orient before quitting and looking after Walsall for a short spell. His always controversial career might have landed him up in Greece, and it was Colchester's extreme good fortune that he chose Layer Road.

Dick was an utterly innovative manager – he once had flowers placed in the West Brom dressing room – and was invariably in the news delighting the media.

There was a now largely forgotten incident when Orient were involved in a thoroughly bad-tempered match at Layer Road. It was a 2-2 draw and there was an unseemly brawl when the players trooped off. Graham, trying to intervene in a clash between Orient's Terry Bradbury and a spectator was punched by angry Colchester fans.

That fleeting interlude was, however, a distant memory; Graham earned immortal fame with the cup win over Leeds and was unquestionably Layer Road's most revered and most loved manager.

There was a lot more to it than Leeds and the Watney Cup, for under Graham there was never a dull moment. There was his imposing presence and iron-fist training routines, and he always came up with a good story for the press boys.

He began with a rash of signings, many of them London-based, including pint-sized Terry Dyson who starred in Spurs' wonder double season; Brian Wood and Danny Light from Palace; Owen Simpson from Orient and Brian Gibbs for a bargain £4,000 from Gillingham. I well remember a lot of these players cheekily making separate taxi trips from Colchester North Station on training days, eyed by the cynical Graham who made appropriate disdainful comments.

The lively Light did well with 12 goals as U's finished in sixth spot just outside the promotion frame but they did little of note in the cup, beaten 1-0 at home by unfancied Exeter City who earned a plum tie against Manchester United in the process.

As revealed, Graham had an impish sense of humour, and there was often an twinkle in his eyes disguising the bluff exterior. The Exeter defeat threw up a humorous incident. Newly signed right-winger Barry Rowan from Millwall had arrived with a big reputation, but he had a dreadful match and was to be singled out for Dick's lashing tongue in the dressing room. However, there was power failure which prompted Dick to light a candle in search of poor Rowan, who had rapidly departed, coat over playing kit, to the club house where he resided next to the ground. Rowan was not to live there for long. He played only three games before leaving for Reading.

The same club house was later to be occupied by goalkeeper Tony Macedo, a flamboyant character who had performed at top level for Fulham. He liked to play the horses and turned out for 40 games and then dramatically quit the country overnight for South Africa to play for Durban City.

To help in rebuilding, Graham sold Trevis to Walsall for £10,000 and Forbes to Norwich for £9,000. The new players who then came in included striker Roy Massey from Orient, Micky Brown (Luton) and Ken Jones (ex-Millwall and Southend).

Jones, an elegant mover and good finisher, proved an instant hit, scoring 5 goals in his first 9 games and later 10 in 8. His big moments came in the League Cup ties against the strong Birmingham side of the day. At Layer Road, Jones scored in a 1-1 draw and in the St Andrews replay put the U's ahead before a 17,000 crowd. Colchester looked through until the Blues desperately scrambled home with goals by Geoff Vowden and Phil Summerhill, both laid on by a then sixteen-year-old Trevor Francis.

These creditable performances have always been dwarfed by later momentous events which, unfortunately for him, Jones did not figure. He was injury-plagued and missed out on Leeds. In all, he played 84 games in a U's shirt and scored 27 goals before moving to Margate.

In this eventful 1970/71 season came the three most significant signings – Ray Crawford, Dave Simmons and Brian Lewis. The last-named duo cost big money at the turn of the year, but proved to be a wonderful investment. Simmons was a snip from Aston Villa, big and bustling. Lewis, a much-travelled skilful forward, had come from Luton. Both scored on their Boxing Day debut against Lincoln City and never looked back.

The peerless Crawford had already made his mark and was the most amazing footballer I have ever encountered, and one of the few players who have basked in two top-line careers. What a master stroke it was when Graham forked out £4,000 for him from non-League Kettering. Ray was thirty-three, had a milk round, and was effectively on soccer's scrapheap but Graham had a knack of reviving fading careers.

Nine years earlier, Crawford had been a headline wonder boy, a scoring sensation in Ipswich Town's astonishing First Division Championship triumph in 1961/62, and the then Town boss, Alf Ramsey, twice picked him for England.

Crawford reappeared as good as ever and was to make even bigger headlines. He was cheery, optimistic and cockily confident – a natural winner, as befitted a former guerrilla fighter in Malaya. He was dubbed 'Jungle Boy'! A good ball player, Ray was a brilliant header of the ball and a fine poacher, and what with the smallness of Layer Road, he loved to chat to the crowd. He was just a swagger away from being one of the all-time greats.

The famous Leeds victory was preceded by events largely forgotten. There was a first-round win over non-League Ringmer – 3-0, with Crawford bagging them all – and Cambridge United also fell 3-0 at Layer Road.

The next hurdle was far from easy, though – bonny non-Leaguers Barnet on their sloping Underhill pitch. The tie had been postponed from Saturday, and it was still a skating rink and an utter lottery. All in all, Colchester did well to win a tricky affair, ultimately decided by a Mick Mahon free-kick special. Graham wasn't happy over the conditions and standing on the iron-hard pitch said, 'These ties cannot be called a contest of skill. If we are going to play on pitches like this, we will have to pad up players they way they do in American football. I'm just happy we didn't have any injuries.'

Rochdale, then a more than handy outfit and well supported, were no less easy at Spotlands which was a well-populated venue that day with a 12,000-plus crowd. Frankly they looked set to repeat their giant-killing win over Coventry in the previous round. When 3-1 down, U's seemed well past the point of no return but dramatically came back from the dead to square at 3-3. I recall meeting up with fans at Manchester who had left early convinced that Colchester had lost. They just didn't believe the result.

Crawford had headed the opener from the tightest of angles but Rochdale took command. The closing stages produced sizzling action. Bobby Cram missed a penalty in the 67th minute but Graham switched Lewis into the middle and, with seven minutes left, he scored. Then Crawford dummied a Hall cross and Simmons levelled.

They were still playing the Great Escape when the fifth-round draw was made amid much excitement. It was still a broadcast affair and happy Colchester players were pictured listening in. Dick Graham, however, never got excited over these occasions. He heard the news when in the toilet!

The incentive to beat Rochdale was immense. Leeds United at Layer Road – the mind boggled! Don Revie's troops were world famous. The previous season they had been beaten finalists, losing to Chelsea after a 2-2 draw. They had also lost in 1965 to Liverpool and were long overdue for a Wembley victory and with their array of stars were strong odds-on favourites.

The Rochdale replay produced a 5-0 win and a display which I still rank today as the most professional and near perfect ninety minutes by any Colchester team. It was a wet night but there was a 11,205 crowd and, on a mud heap, U's were like a well-oiled machine and played their opponents off the park. Lewis and Simmons started the romp and exciting wing back Brian Hall was devastating, forcing an own goal via one of his sizzling crosses. Then he laid on one for Crawford before Mahon came up with one of his spectaculars. It was all utterly breathtaking, and the watching Revie must have been impressed.

The build up to the match saw the familiar gimmickry and U's were headline news. There wasn't a day when Graham and Crawford and the players were not being pictured and interviewed.

There were seven players over the age of thirty and someone termed them 'Graham's Granddads', whilst Dick's favourite reading matter was said to be tales of scaling Everest. He himself said he would climb the Colchester Castle walls if U's won.

The biggest kidding came from Crawford. He teased and taunted big Jack Charlton, calling him his rabbit. He scored a hat-trick at Elland Road and another in the return season when Ipswich ruled the roost. I'm sure that the Crawford bravado stuff was inspired by Graham. Ray also went on record that he owed his new success to Graham's tough training programme. He said, 'Don Revie was right when he says we are the fittest team he has seen. Dick works us really hard and the first day I experienced I thought I was going to die.'

The players trained at Holland-on-Sea, and part of the build up was a dip in a freezing North Sea. They stayed in what was called their lucky hotel and Graham put a ban on them talking about the game. There were no other restrictions and in fact the team were allowed to stay up to watch the late-night TV film, as it starred their favourite, John Wayne.

Meantime, at Layer Road, there was a spot check conducted by Sir Walter Winterbottom and his ground safety team of experts. Winterbottom, former England team manager, was determined to prevent any further disasters following the Ibrox affair in which sixty-six fans died only a month earlier. U's were chosen because of their crowd-pulling fixture and the ground was passed on all counts.

The day of the match, Saturday 13 February 1971, Graham spent the morning on his own looking out over the water and said afterwards he was convinced Colchester would win. It was something of a Churchillian touch and it could have been Winston looking out over the Channel for inspiration on the eve of the Battle of Britain.

So to the match which became such a historic occasion that people still remember where they were that day. Just as in 1948 against Huddersfield and Bradford PA, a packed Layer Road was all excitement and animation, a splendid vista you would have loved to preserve for all time.

My main memories remain: Big Jack Charlton so nerve-wracked he conceded a corner with a back pass from around the halfway line; the amazing goals that put U's three up; Crawford clean through and all set to make it four when his legs gave way through sheer exhaustion; the 16,000 crowd's perpetual roar and the cries of 'easy, easy'; Leeds' late rally and Graham Smith's sensational reflex save to deny Mick Jones the equaliser. Right from the outset, Colchester set the pace and Leeds' anxiety when Charlton dumped Simmons on his backside near the left flank touchline; Lewis floating his free-kick cross beautifully. In the packed penalty area, it simply had to be Crawford's head winning the day.

The second goal was bizarre, something like a *Keystone Cops* comedy scene filmed in very slow motion. Crawford, Sprake and Leeds' defenders were all grounded, and Crawford stretched out a leg for the ball to crawl into the net, Simmons following up to make sure.

The third goal in the 56th minute began with Crawford way back in defence. He played the ball wide to Lewis, whose long cross sped in like an arrow, and caught Paul Reaney and Sprake in two minds. Big Simmons timed it all to perfection, headed home, and pandemonium broke loose. Again, from the Leeds angle, there was a touch of tragic comedy about it all. Colchester were in no way flattered by their lead. They had man-marked brilliantly, had taken the game to the opposition and Mahon had been devastating with his pacy runs.

But the Leeds fightback came, started by iron man Norman Hunter who headed in a short corner from Johnny Giles. With fifteen minutes left, Giles slammed in another and it was a grandstand nail-biting finish with Smith's late wonder-save. U's breathlessly hung on and Dick Graham, amid all the back-slapping and celebrations had time to say 'Leeds finished by playing the best and most controlled football I have ever seen'.

The game was BBC's *Match of the Day* and the commentator was David Coleman. Those memorable goals are in the archives forever and keep cropping up on television when cup time comes around.

The unlucky U's player was Ken Jones who, but for an chipped ankle bone, would have probably been in the action. But Ken still played a major role. He was sent north to spy on Leeds and came back with this report: 'Too many First Division teams are afraid of them. Attack them, harry them at the back and you can win.'

The publicity afterwards was out of this world. Every national newspaper, and there were a lot more in those days, lauded Graham and Colchester to the skies. The London *Evening Standard*, first on the streets, had a banner front page headline: 'One. Two. Three. Leeds Are Out' and on Sunday, the *News of the World* proclaimed 'Crawford's Crackers!'.

Some sports writers had to eat their words, especially two *Sun* pundits, Frank Clough and Peter Batt, who had written: 'Effort, enthusiasm and determination can take you far but not all the way. Leeds may have to survive a fright especially in the early stages when it will appear the stand is coming down about their ears. But when the final whistle goes there will be only one winner.'

Batt forecast on the eve of the match, 'The brutal difference lies in the class of player. I wouldn't be surprised to see Crawford pop one in before Leeds settle. But the final score cast must be Colchester 1, Leeds 3'.

Frank Nicklin, also in the *Sun* had suggested that Colchester and Brentford shouldn't be in the FA Cup. Graham's response was, 'It was obviously a controversial article, but it worked the other way for me. It probably made my players even more determined to prove we have every right to be in the cup.'

One had to salute the dignity in defeat of Don Revie, one of the true gentlemen of the game. Cigar butts around where he sat bore testimony to the tension and he said afterwards, 'There are no excuses. Colchester didn't play above themselves. They are a very difficult side to beat. They played well and that's the story of the match.'

So the champagne corks popped and everyone celebrated, stories abounding in the national and local papers. Thirty-four-year-old Brian Gibbs, who described himself as just a bread-and-butter player said, 'It was champagne till three on Sunday morning and in the pub yesterday lunchtime, I could have got drunk three times over if I had accepted all offers.'

Brian Hall said, 'I'm still shaking. It was fantastic', and John Gilchrist, who man-marked Giles so effectively that he was having treatment to bruised legs, said 'Norman Hunter was their best player. Without him, we would have got six.'

Crawford's phone never stopped ringing and he spoke in glowing terms of his wife and three daughters who were his greatest fans, 'I have been on top in my career before, but Saturday was an experience I will never forget.' He added, 'Did I celebrate? Like a director. I have been made director of my local pub side the Olive Leaves, and I went out with the club for a slap-up dinner at an Ipswich nightclub. Who next? I would like Liverpool at Layer Road – we have no one to fear now.'

Thousands of words have been spilled over the biggest shock game of them all and it remains today a frequent topic for discussion. After all, that Leeds team would today have been Champions League material and make no mistake, Charlton, Lorimer, Giles, Hunter and Clarke were veritable giants of the game.

There was, of course, no Billy Bremner, who was sidelined by injury, and it was continually argued by Leeds that he could have made all the difference. Certainly this flamboyant firebrand would not have taken kindly to the way events went but even without him Leeds were world-class.

A few years back, I took part in a BBC radio quiz marking the big game. Ray Crawford, looking as dapper as ever, and John Kurila were the U's men involved. It was good fun but I have a hunch that the shock defeat and humiliation still rankled with the Leeds players and the view was that had the game been played another ten times, Leeds would never have been beaten.

That's probably true, but nothing can ever be taken away from a Colchester side who defeated one of the best teams in Europe. It was, as most soccer writers said, a welcome whiff of fresh air and proved that the last legs of romance and humanity had not yet been drained from the great competition. As Donald Saunders of the *Daily Telegraph* said, 'In these drab days when a footballers action seems always to be prompted by cold commercial instinct, it was like the first breath of spring to watch the Colchester players gallop over to their manager and lift him shoulder high at the final whistle.'

Talking of romance, the other fifth-round ties that wonderful afternoon were magnetic too and some wide-eyed optimists were even daydreaming of an all-East Anglian final as Ipswich Town was still involved, drawing at Stoke. But unaccountably, they lost the replay and failed to make the last eight. It was the impossible dream, of course.

And so for Everton and already the game had caught the imagination. Roger Heywood in the *Sun* conducted a poll among fans and came up with the conclusion that ninety-one per cent would like to see Graham's granddads thrash Everton, but only seven per cent wanted Colchester to win the semi-final.

As a Chelsea fan put it, 'The cup final is the soccer showpiece of the year. It must never be reduced to farce by some tiddler from the Fourth Division sneaking in to make it a big belly laugh'. Heywood's retort was 'A belly laugh to you sir. You are talking rubbish. If Colchester could pull off the soccer sensation of all time. it would be the greatest thing that ever happened in English football.'

By now, soccer and Everton was the sole topic of conversation and U's were honoured with a civic reception at Colchester Castle. It was a splendid affair, with MP Anthony Buck and the Mayor Richard Wheeler in attendance. The guests included 'Digger Kettle' of the 1948 giant-killers. Mr Buck said if Everton were beaten, there could well be a House of Commons reception. There was a good-luck telegram from Leeds, and Dick Graham flew north to see Everton play Manchester United. What days they were.

The Everton Experience

Views were mixed when the exciting sixth-round draw decreed it was away to Everton. It would be tough of course but a huge crowd was assured and the payout would be good. The Colchester players were on an attendance-based bonus – £150 for every 1,000 while the club could expect to rake in £10,000.

The broadcast draw saw Dick Graham lock himself in his office. He said, 'I never listen to the draw. It's just one of those things. I like it to creep upon me. I am not worried about it and I like to take these sort of things day by day.'

The sixth round meant Merseyside was set to go soccer mad as Liverpool were also at home against Spurs. The other ties saw Leicester City paired with Arsenal and Hull City taking on Stoke and many bookmakers made Everton favourites to win the cup, quoting Colchester at 200-1.

People were still enthusing over the Leeds game and Brian Lewis was, in a lot of critics' eyes, the Man of the Match despite Crawford's goals.

Lewis, the most gifted of ball payers and a busy operator, certainly played a key role. His sleight of foot and control gave experienced England defender Terry Cooper a torrid ninety minutes and his superbly lobbed crosses laid on goals for Crawford and Simmons.

Lewis was a wanderlust player, always in search of first-team football. He owned a wry sense of humour and had plied his trade with Crystal Palace, Portsmouth, Coventry, Luton and Oxford, with varying degrees of success. Initially, he was reluctant to come to Layer Road. But he said later, 'It is great. We stay at the best hotels and travel well. I'm happy to settle here.'

Just as it was prior to Leeds, there was plenty of ballyhoo and daily press coverage. As always, Dick Graham explored every avenue, trying to turn anything to his advantage. He really was a thinking manager. He said, 'Records show that surprisingly few teams get through this sixth round at the first attempt. It encourages us even though everyone seems to have written us off. Perhaps Everton will suffer because our game does not have the same aura of importance as the Liverpool v. Spurs game'. He went on, 'If Everton don't win, it will be years before they live it down. All these things can count in our favour as long as we give what we gave against Leeds.'

The training was again at Holland-on-Sea, the team staying at their lucky hotel. There were whispers of possible team changes and John Gilchrist who had man-marked John Giles so brilliantly was still under treatment for an Achilles injury. Micky Cook, then a fledgling nineteen-year-old, was spoken as a possible replacement and Ken Jones was also in the squad.

Cook had been snapped up from Leyton Orient. He must rue even today missing out on such a momentous occasion, but he went onto become one of the club's immortals with a record number of appearances, 695 in League and cup between 1969 and 1984.

Micky, who started out as a winger, was Colchester United through and through and remains so as director of youth football. He was redoubtable, a dependable full-back with an attacking streak, and he amazingly scored 22 League goals and 3 in Cup games.

All the time Crawford was making optimistic noises and hogging the headlines. He was now writing regularly for the *Sun* and was upbeat at the prospect of meeting Everton. He said, 'Last time I played against them was for Ipswich and I scored the best and worst goals of my career. The worst was when I knocked the ball out of Gordon West's reach with my hand and into the net. The referee didn't see it and Everton were furious.'

Everton were, of course, a club with a tremendous tradition. In the 1930 Dixie Dean era, they had won the First Division Championship and the cup in successive seasons and were First Division Champions again in 1938/39. Post-war they were Wembley winners against Sheffield Wednesday in 1965/66 and went into the U's match as First Division Champions the previous season. The squad bristled with big names and was highly priced. With the backing of pools magnate John Moores, they had the big spenders tag by spending over £500,000 on players.

Best known by far was Alan Ball, an England World Cup hero of 1966, who cost £110,000 from Blackpool. He had over forty caps. Most of the team were Under-23 internationals. There was full-back Keith Newton, and powerhouse wing half Howard Kendall, who came from Preston for £80,000. He had played for them at Wembley, the youngest to do so when aged seventeen.

The main striker was big Joe Royle, 6ft plus and thirteen stone, who was one of the best headers in the game. A nice twist was that he and U's 'keeper Graham Smith both played for the same school, Quarry Street Grammar. When an Everton scout came along, Graham prayed he was looking for a goalkeeper, but he took Joe instead. Smith said, 'On Saturday, I'll have to make sure he does not have me diving the wrong way'.

Likeable Graham, who had three A levels and seven O levels and was qualified as a PE teacher, had another sentimental reason for going back to his native Liverpool – his father was a devout Everton fan and a season ticket holder who had first taken him to Goodison as a starry-eyed kid. Smith senior said he would be cheering on Colchester.

So to the big day, Saturday 6 March 1971. There was massed support from Essex with three special trains, a fleet of coaches and three aircraft from Stanstead. In all, it was reckoned that 8,000 people made the trip. There had been snow in the North but a slow thaw meant there was never a threat of a postponement. It was a tremendous occasion. Sixth-round day is always something special and here we had Liverpool playing Spurs on the other side of town at Anfield. As the legions of fans began to assemble that crisp cold Saturday full of expectancy, one felt the tug of excitement when taking in the awesome grandeur of a packed Goodison. The official gate was 53,028 people, the second-largest gathering any Colchester team have ever confronted.

The match alas was another of those anti-climax affairs. Invariably when it came to big clubs away, Colchester found it beyond them. But the 5-0 scoreline could never have been predicted in the first twenty-five minutes. Colchester took the game to their opposition and hopes ran high. Everton had to defend to keep out Mick Mahon and inevitably Crawford was sniffing for goals. Andy Rankin, a surprise late choice for West, had to be at full stretch to keep out one Crawford effort and brilliantly cut out a menacing Lewis cross. Then came the slaughter as Everton suddenly clicked with four goals in a devastating thirteen-minute spell. Smith had already made blinding saves from Ball and Henry Newton but he was beaten on twenty-three minutes when Kendall headed in a crisp free-kick by Ball.

It was then that Colchester completely 'lost it' as Graham describes in more detail in another chapter. A slick combination of passes saw Kendall score with a half-hit shot and when Kurila dallied over a clearance, Royle lobbed a third goal from twenty-five yards. On thirty-four minutes, that slick winger Jimmy Husband went through the middle and drove home a spectacular fourth, and U's were dead and buried. It was all so similar to the breathtaking Blackpool goal burst in 1948.

To Colchester's credit, they held out until the 83rd minute when the silky Ball got his name on the scoresheet. Over the last twenty minutes, U's in fact had looked the more likely scorers, Crawford hitting a post and Lewis having one blocked. In hindsight too, the scoreline was a little flattering. In between their golden moments, Everton were patchy and indifferent. As always, U's had a good national press and trooped off Goodison to a well-deserved long-standing ovation. It was as much an overall tribute for their entire cup-run achievement.

Graham's first response was to say, 'That 5-0 scoreline is a bit harsh. I did not think Everton were five goals better. They were quicker than we were and we were fine while we could play at our own pace.' He added, 'We came here to play our usual attacking game, and in the first twenty minutes, we could have had a goal and then the game might have gone either way.' Everton's Harry Catterick's opposite view was that 'Colchester were much as we expected and I felt we should have had more goals, but the pitch was bumpy when it cut up'.

Don Evans in the *News of the World* wrote 'Colchester kept coming back time and again and they certainly had nothing to be ashamed of.' Don Hardisty in the *Sunday Express* said, 'The giant-killing season is over. All Colchester were able to salvage were a golden handshake from the gate and an international class rating for Graham Smith for at least five more goals which his brilliant goalkeeping prevented.'

Again in hindsight I believe that Dick Graham still has recriminations over his tactics and his inability to communicate with his players at a crucial stage of the game, and he should have adopted a more defensive policy instead of going for the jugular. I also believe he pondered long over making a team change. Whatever, the great run was over, and the romantics had had their day. The travelling exodus were well behaved and it was all great fun while it lasted.

Graham though was not happy over what he called 'Everton's pettiness and gamesmanship' saying, 'The gesture of the Everton players in clapping my side off at the end was wonderful and deserved. But I didn't like the other things that happened up there. We were not given the normal courtesy of providing the visiting teams with footballs for them to warm up with in the dressing rooms.'

He was even more forthright when he declared: 'I think it was pettiness from such a big club. I also think it was gamesmanship. I wonder how Everton are treated when they go away.' So much ill feeling was abroad and Graham also complained about the Colchester mascot who was not allowed to change into his outfit in the dressing room as he usually did and he accused Catterick of not seeing him before or after the match.

Catterick denied all the accusations: 'I am surprised Dick has taken this attitude. There is no truth in the suggestion that we indulged in gamesmanship before or during the game, unless you call scoring five goals as over-professionalism' was his response.

Two of the other ties, including the Liverpool–Spurs affray, ended goalless, Leicester and Arsenal also a stalemate. Everton fell to Liverpool in the semi-finals and Arsenal ended the Wembley winners.

The back-to-normality angle underlined the vivid contrasts between top and bottom. In midweek after Goodison, Everton played Greek aces Panathinaikos in the European Cup. And on the Monday, U's met humble Darlington at Layer Road. They showed no reaction, winning 2-0 before a crowd of 7,110 with goals by Crawford and Simmons. There was a whiff of promotion in the air but a shaky run in led to an ultimate sixth position. It was cruelly disappointing for Dick Graham but he had another headline sensation up his sleeve for everyone to marvel over.

Watney Wonders

The season 1971/72 had an exciting and unique prelude – the Watney Cup, a sponsored money-spinner that featured the highest scoring sides of the previous season and no offsides outside the penalty box.

U's just qualified and in the opening rounds disposed of two very good sides, Luton Town and Carlisle, before winning the final against First Division power men West Bromwich Albion in an amazing penalty shoot-out – so Colchester at last won a prestige national trophy.

The only downside was that it was accomplished without Ray Crawford. He played against Luton but then negotiated a move to South African club Durban City whom goalkeeper Tony Macedo had joined earlier. It was sad that Crawford left under a cloud and a bust up with the man who had resurrected his career.

Crawford complained of being treated like a leper and had not been invited to the banquet that followed the Watney triumph. Dick Graham's angry response was sharp. He said, 'He left us in the lurch. I did everything to get him away to Durban on time despite the fact he had a contract here. He earned more than £3,000 from us last season but he goes around telling people we are not paying him a living wage.' In all, Crawford played 35 games in U's colours and scored 31 goals. He was a one-season marvel and will forever be remembered for Leeds.

Back to the Watney Mann sponsored competition, an excellent pipe-opener to a campaign and with goals aplenty it was popular, U's opening games commanding bigger gates than they would have done for a friendly. Luton, then in the Second Division, were beaten by a Brian Lewis penalty, and Lewis was again the star of the show in the 2-0 victory over Carlisle. Brian Gibbs with a dipping thirty-yard volley and Lewis with a header from Mick Mahon's cross got the goals and there was only one offside in the entire ninety minutes.

So to West Brom in the final. They were one of Graham's former clubs and Colchester were presented with a chance of avenging the Hawthorns FA Cup defeat of 1968 which they did in style in a quite remarkable match viewed by a mammoth TV audience estimated at twelve million. Commentator Barry Davies stated, 'It was one of the most fantastic and historic matches ever played in this country.'

He was arguably right – a see-saw eight-goal thriller, a West Brom equaliser in the last minute and then England's first ever penalty shoot-out, something that was to start a completely new vogue.

Mind you, not everybody concurred. Some smart-alec writers likened it all to the silly season and something akin to *Monty Python's Flying Circus* or *It's A Knockout*. And, of course, even today when the penalty shoot-out again featured prominently in the World Cup, there are folk who dislike it intensely and still feel there should be a better way to decide a game.

At the time of the Watney Cup, Graham had no doubts. He said, 'Penalties are one of the skills and arts of the game for the taker and the goalkeeper.' The final, viewed by 18,487 fans, was all action. I could never understand why Aston Villa and Birmingham played in a local derby friendly a few miles away. That attracted 36,000 and obviously affected the Hawthorns turn out. Surely Villa could have altered the kick-off time.

Eight of the United team that beat Leeds played, the other three being Eric Burgess (a signing from Watford), Brian Owen (a classy performer later to be trainer, and a top Layer Road medic and coach), and stripling Phil Bloss (little did he know would be the storybook hero).

The ninety minutes were frenzied to say the least. There was a disallowed Jeff Astle goal before Mick Mahon opened the scoring. Then Len Cantello, from twenty-five yards, and Astle, from a narrow angle, made it 2-1; Dave Simmons squared at 2-2 only for Colin Suggett's cheeky back-heeler to put Albion ahead again.

It looked good for the high-priced Baggies at this point but U's turned this thriller on its head with some superb attacking football. Mahon, playing the game of his life, struck a sizzling thirty-yard leveller and when Lewis stroked home a late penalty after John Kaye had floored Mahon, it looked all over. But with the seconds ticking away, Astle kneed the ball over the line to make it 4-4 and bring the fans flooding on the pitch.

The shoot out was dramatic and prolonged white-knuckle stuff. Today they are commonplace but then it was quite sensational. It had the crowd breathless. Twice, kicks had to be retaken as the respective keepers had moved. At the end, Albion missed twice, Ray Wilson and Cantello firing over while Jim Cumbes saved from Bobby Cram.

So to the final drama. When it came to the last kick, the seventeen-year old Bloss begged for the chance and then calmly scored. 'I just fancied my chance and wanted to make up for my error that gave them their first goal' he confessed afterwards and Graham's team selection was justified.

Bloss had previously played only one first-team game, celebrating with a debut goal. Oddly enough, his career was later uneventful. He made thirty-four appearances and his main claim to fame apart from the Watney winner was to marry Graham's daughter and become a highly successful estate agent.

Albion's defeat hurt their fans. They had only just welcomed new manager Don Howe, who himself was most downcast. I recall too many of those supporters openly weeping over the indignity of losing a prestige game to a Fourth Division club.

Colchester travelled back to Essex in style with the handsome trophy with a police motorcycle escort from the ground to Birmingham station. Skipper Cram, a former Albion player, made a fascinating observation when he said 'Did you know Colchester had never scored a goal on a First Division ground before today? Now we have to score eight to win a match.'

Cram had come to Layer Road from Vancouver Royals and he later went back to Canada. He was an inspiring skipper and a steely performer. In many people's eyes, the final was Mahon's best-ever and Mick himself said, 'Definitely my most memorable exciting game, more so than Leeds and my debut as a teenager for Newcastle against Middlesbrough when I scored and made another.'

Mahon, a dashing eye-catching winger, was simply devastating on his day. He was a former amateur international whose career was going nowhere when he was signed from York City. He ended on a high note too when in 1974 he moved to Wimbledon, shining at top level.

Colchester continued to roll out the Watney barrel for some days. There was a celebration town procession and another castle banquet. They were feted also with the presentation of a giant-killer's cup presented by a Sunday national paper.

U's were the talk of the country. Once more they had struck a blow for the little clubs and added a touch of fun to a predictable game. I worked it out about that time that in two years, they had, including replays, played seventeen national cup ties, four of them against First Division clubs, four against Second and four against Third Division. Of these seventeen games, they had ten victories, three draws and only four defeats.

The Watney Cup in the boardroom sideboard – everyone expected promotion but it was far from beer and skittles, as the inconsistent season ended in a mid-table eleventh placing. Too many home points were dropped and just a year on after Leeds there was a first-round cup defeat 4-1 against Shrewsbury – at home too!

More was promised in the League Cup with Brentford and Swindon beaten, setting up a third round tie at Blackpool – shades of 1948. For the first time ever, the team flew – a fifty-minute flight from Stanstead. Some of the players were apprehensive and Dave Simmons was, I recall, quite petrified. Supporters aplenty made the trip, also taking in the illuminations, but Blackpool dimmed U's lights, winning, 4-0.

By the end of the season, many of the Leeds heroes had departed – Cram, Garvey, Gibbs, Gilchrist, Kurila, Lewis and Smith following on the heels of Crawford. And we saw the start of a new era with a lot of youngsters making their mark, notably Steve Leslie, Steve Foley and Lindsay Smith.

Graham Smith, one of the club's best-ever goalkeepers, kept the West Brom link going, leaving for the Hawthorns for what many thought was an underpriced £10,000. Gilchrist and Garvey went non-League but that controversial character John Kurila signed for Lincoln City.

John was the most misunderstood of footballers. He was a ferocious tackler and hard man and his very name was fearsome. When at Northampton, he once so aroused an irate visiting lady supporter, that at half-time near the tunnel, she poured a cup of tea all over him. But John, for all his reputation, was extremely mild-mannered away from the action.

John, of Lithuanian descent and Scottish born, was kicking a ball about in the Gorbals as a kid. He reached the top when starring in the Northampton side that indulged in the dizzy heights of the First Division for just one memorable season, which included a goal-less draw against Liverpool. John played 20 games in the top flight and was certainly one of Graham's snip signings.

The 1972/73 season began badly with only two wins in the first two months. It was largely due to finances and a very young side, and it all led to the sensational events at the annual meeting of shareholders when Graham dropped a bombshell by resigning.

The whole affair was a travesty. A police sergeant, forty-four-year-old Alan Frost, whose five shares in the club had ironically been won in a raffle, suddenly made a personal attack on Graham over his management after a record £23,000 profit had been reported.

Graham was shattered. I had always suspected that under the often gruff exterior he was highly sensitive. Immediate efforts were made to make him change his mind but to no avail. Later he spoke to the press at length and told the *Evening Gazette*, 'The football manager is the world's Aunt Sally. I was on trial at that annual meeting. I didn't go with the intention of resigning but suddenly the business part of the meeting was over and I looked up and there it was – the stage was set for the trial of Dick Graham.'

Graham gives a fuller version of those unhappy events in another chapter. Certainly, the whole wretched business left a rotten taste. I wrote in the *Colchester Express*, 'No-one stood up to support Graham with a vote of confidence and in any event, what was he supposed to be defending in the first place?'

In an opinion piece, I also penned, 'Boardrooms everywhere will surely be suddenly wary in the future of allowing shares to be won in raffles. They might find themselves in the unfortunate position Colchester United found themselves in and other men with no obvious claims to headlines might be tempted to win dubious immortality in the events of football club affairs.'

The entire football world was in shock over Graham's resignation. He was, after all, a national soccer figure and Don Revie and Bobby Robson, the then Ipswich boss, expressed their regret, speaking of the sad loss to football.

Graham left a young promising side, and less than twenty-four hours after the fatal meeting, they whacked Crewe 5-1 at Layer Road to give their answer to the shock events. They obviously played that one for the manager. The odd thing was that Frost, the man who produced the shock, was unrepentant. He told reporters, 'There is nothing personal in what happened. I just voiced my opinion as an individual; I don't think Dick Graham is a good manager and I said so. It came as a shock when Graham said what he did.'

Graham had resigned before but changed his mind after the then chairman Bill Graver, with whom he often disagreed, left the club. This time, it was for good. Sadly and so unnecessarily, a momentous era ended.

4

Top Boss

The Legend

He relaxed in his chair and began to reminisce. Dick Graham, the man they call the legend, is in his early eighties. He is not so good on his feet maybe. But there is still a twinkle in the eyes, the brain is alert and the soccer memory crystal clear.

A fund of stories begin to flow and the Don Revie connection keeps cropping up. The pair first met when they were youngsters playing for Leicester City, Don eventually signing for Manchester City and Dick for Crystal Palace – for them a then record fee for a goalkeeper.

In 1964/65 their paths crossed again as managers. Graham had done wonderfully well for Palace and they had a fine FA Cup run that took them to the sixth round, their opponents fittingly enough Revie's Leeds.

Palace were the form team and favourites but the game was snowed off and as Dick recalls, 'I'm convinced that had it been played then we would have won. It went ahead in midweek and we were off the boil. I made a couple of changes and things rebounded. They scored two quick goals and won 3-0.' Dick remembers going to see Revie in their dressing room to congratulate him and he was in tears crying with relief.'

'That and Leeds always stuck in my mind and I thought if ever the chance came again I would be the one crying' Graham observed. Fate indeed decreed that it happened years on.

After the Palace defeat, Graham says the disappointment was so intense that he was given the cold shoulder so much that he thought he had contracted a contagious disease. Within months he had gone and Bert Head was the new manager. The story underlines the ups and downs of Graham's career. Even at Colchester, he might have left within a couple of weeks of arriving following a petty row over painting the dressing room.

The Layer Road memories naturally enough are mostly Leeds and the revelation of the main tactics. Talk to Graham and it's as if the match was only yesterday. The chief ploy was man-marking John Gilchrist on schemer John Giles, and John Kurila on striker Alan Clarke. There was also the plan to get in continual crosses and with Dave Simmons keeping Jack Charlton occupied, suspect Gary Sprake's confidence might be undermined.

Until the last tension-loaded minutes, it all worked and the goals came from crosses, one from Brian Gibbs and two from the wily Brian Lewis, the second, amazingly hit from around the halfway line, certainly caught out the hapless Sprake. Then there is the Graham premonition story at Holland-on-Sea before the big game. As he says, 'For February, it was a beautiful morning more like summer. I had given my last team talks and some of the lads were on the beach with a ball. We were all relaxed and it's a funny thing about life that not for the first time, I had this premonition from out of the blue that we would win.'

Graham's heroes are now widely-scattered but he frequently contacts them. Graham Smith is in America; Bobby Cram in Vancouver and Brian Garvey down-under in Australia. Alas, John Gilchrist, Brian Hall and Lewis all passed on, Lewis at a tragically early age. The rest are in England, all semi-retired. Brian Gibbs is in Bedfordshire where he does a lot of voluntary work; Kurila is in Northampton, the town where he began his main soccer career; Ray Crawford resides in Portsmouth and Mick Mahon runs a guest house in Ipswich. Dave Simmons is in nearby Cambridge. Not so long ago Garvey, looking fit and well, dropped in at Layer Road for the pre-season friendly matches.

Dick professes to have no favourites but I have an idea Gibbs occupies a special place. He was his most expensive signing – £4,000 from Gillingham. 'Gibby' was a player who, for years, got 15 to 20 goals a season and 'you could rely on that', Graham observed.

Simmons and Lewis cost £3,500 each and were bargains. Crawford was a snip from Kettering and Graham reflects, 'I tried to get him when he was at Charlton but just missed out. He came to us on £30 a week and after he had scored 30 goals in just half a season in the Southern League, I was sure of him.'

Inevitably we come to the Leeds sequel, the quarter-finals and Everton. Was Dick Graham really visualising Wembley? He says not but remains utterly convinced that had the game been at Layer Road, U's would have won. The fact the he was unable to communicate from the touchline was the main factor.

Goodison Park with 50,000 spectators is awesome and as Dick says, 'I do feel that the big crowd and the volume of noise were big factors. Some of the players simply lost it and I couldn't get any instructions out on the field to them. I was praying for someone to go down injured so I could get a message on with trainer Dennis Mochan, but you couldn't get to the players and they were used to hearing my voice from the touchline.'

The other factor Dick believes influenced the match was his tactics. He encouraged his players to go for it. He says, 'I don't think my team could have played defensive football. They were so attack-minded. We had so many players who could score – Crawford, Gibbs, Lewis, Mahon Simmons and Brian Hall. Of course we could well have had a goal in the first twenty minutes. How do you play for a draw anyway?'

Having said that, he admitted that Everton played some great football on the day. They had been on a bit of a low, changed the goalkeeper and were on very good money to win. There was a big contrast with Colchester as Dick relates, 'I suddenly discovered there was nothing in the players contracts, or mine for that, about reaching the quarter-finals. After talks with the chairman, it was agreed it would be gauged on the gate – 50p for every 1,000. That meant £70, but Everton were getting thousands.'

Graham returns to the communication angle. During his first season, he suddenly decided to stop shouting in a match at Layer Road. At half-time, the players trooped in and a puzzled Bert Howe enquired, 'What's up boss? Are you ill? It's like a morgue out there'.

Graham, often in trouble with referees because of his vocal intrusions, quickly restored to his shouting. As he says, 'They felt at home with it. They didn't object. Indeed it helped them. This was the beauty of the lower divisions. You could get to the players, something you couldn't do at a big club.' After Everton, promotion was looking a certainty and there was no immediate reaction but a freak injury to Simmons in the warm-up before a match proved fatal and, as Lewis was injured in the next game, Graham lost two key players who had gone through an unbeaten run of twelve games.

Simmons' injury more or less ended his career. He was in a plaster cast and as a direct result overbalanced, crashing into a plate-glass door. He was rushed to hospital and lost so much blood, his life was in danger. Graham was convinced Simmons was heading back to the First Division at the time, for a lot of clubs were in for him, but his balance was badly affected and he was never the same player again.

U's had a run of four games without a win and heavy defeats at Notts County and Oldham saw them miss out. Simmons crops up again in an amusing Graham story. About two years back, Anglia TV announced that Dick Graham had died. In fact it was a Norwich newspaperman with the same name. Simmons, distraught at hearing the news, immediately wrote to Dick's wife Anne, expressing his grief. When Graham heard of it all he phoned Simmons and left a message on the answering machine, 'Sorry Dave, the old bugger is not dead yet', he joked.

Graham will not talk too much of that dreadful shareholders meeting that led to his resignation, but he does reveal the work he and trainer Dennis Mochan did behind the scenes to turn things around because it was a difficult time as far as finances were concerned. He said, 'Dennis was great bloke to work with and between us we did everything: the coaching, training and scouting. Things it probably takes ten people to do today.' Graham brought in several youngsters including Steve Leslie, Steve Foley and John McLaughlin and a record profit was made. But this did not seem to influence the meeting and as Dick recalls, 'There were no thanks. It was as if everyone was just waiting for that policeman share-holder to stand up and have a go at me. I suddenly thought "what am I doing here? why am I having to suffer this after working seven days a week not seeing much of my family and not being paid much into the bargain?" He also remembers an elderly pensioner fan who used to come to the ground to see the players train. On a cold day he would be given a hot cup of tea, sometimes with some brandy. Yet this same pensioner stood up at the meeting and offered his criticism too. He thought the players were over-trained and that Mick Mahon was being worn out by taking all the corners. It was laughable – 17 goals came from Mahon's corners that season.

When Graham walked out, there was the Don Revie connection again. Don phoned with his commiserations and said, 'There's a £20 cheque for you in the post and for every week until you get sorted'. Southampton boss Lawrie McMenemy did the same and it illustrated the high respect Graham commanded from fellow managers.

Dick's one-time footballer son-in-law Phil Bloss today lives close at hand. He is in the estate agency business as a freelance. Bloss achieved immortality by taking the decisive penalty in the Watney Cup final and Dick tells of that memorable day, 'I had decided to play Phil although I didn't tell him until the very last minute. He thought he had gone as kit man but he made no mistake from that penalty and having seen him put them away so calmly in reserve games I had no doubts.'

After the shock resignation, Graham never managed a football team again. As he said in the fascinating column he wrote weekly for the *Colchester Express*, 'Now I am just a supporter'.

There followed a short spell running a general store at Alresford and spells at managing sports and leisure centres. Today he enjoys retirement, occasionally watches United games – he had a great reception when a guest for the day – and spends a lot of time relaxing with his charming wife Anne in their West Mersea mobile home.

The Legend lives on. There has surely never been a more innovate controversial and charismatic manager – how the fans, the players and the media miss him.

The Bald Eagle

There was an uplifting of eyebrows when Graham's successor was named as being the unknown Jim Smith, former nondescript player from the lower divisions, who had been running non-League Boston. 'Jim who?' questioned the *Evening Gazette*. But Jim, then thirty-two, a blunt determined Yorkshireman, went on to become one of the best-known and respected managers in the country.

He cut his teeth so successfully at Layer Road that he subsequently managed Blackburn Rovers, Birmingham City, Oxford United, Queens

Park Rangers, Newcastle United, Portsmouth and Derby County. Regularly in the media eye, he remains today one of the wise old birds of the game with always something worthwhile to say. Currently, the much-travelled Smith is back at Portsmouth, number two to Harry Redknapp.

Smith was affectionately dubbed 'The Bald Eagle' but when he came to Colchester, he did have some hair. His CV seemed singularly unimpressive. Sheffield-born, he played 74 games for Aldershot and then went back to Yorkshire with Halifax Town – 114 games. There followed a short spell at Lincoln City before he became player-manager of Boston United.

The story is told that Bobby Robson, then Ipswich boss, upon being shown a list of applicants for the Colchester job by then chairman Roy Chapman immediately pointed to Jim's name as a prime candidate.

Smith started with U's as player-manager, and had a sprinkling of first-team games also turning out for the reserves with great enthusiasm. There was something of a Benny Fenton about him in that he wanted to do everything, take throw-ins, corners and free-kicks, all with a bounding zeal.

Jim was ambitious and set his sights high. One of his big idols was fellow Yorkshireman Geoff Boycott and he possessed much of the famous cricketer's steely grit. The new manager worked exceedingly well with chairman Bob Jackson and with this duo at the helm, Colchester flourished.

Jackson, in my view one of the club's best ever chairmen, ran a large legal practice, but still found time to work exceedingly hard in the U's cause. He was one of Smith's biggest friends and they remain in close touch today. Bob tells many an interesting story of the man who revived the club fortunes in a big way.

Shortly after his arrival, a director asked Smith for a realistic assessment of what Colchester United should be looking to achieve under his leadership. His reply was, 'Win the European Cup of course, but if we miss out on that we should at least be in the Second Division higher than this club has ever been or is ever likely to be.'

At the outset, United finished a perilous third from bottom but in his first full season, Smith got them back to the Third Division. Furthermore, he led an inspired Football League Cup run right to the quarter-finals.

The new boss signed well to supplement the array of young talent Dick Graham had left. His most notable capture was dynamic striker Bobby Svarc from his old club Boston. The names Smith and Svarc will always be synonymous. In the impressive gallery of U's strikers down the years, a portrait of Svarc in scoring pose would always stand supreme. He was not a big fellow, standing only 5ft 7ins but was fearless and scored goals from all distances and angles.

Smith, who paid £6,000 for him, resurrected his career. Bobby drifted into non-League after starting out with Leicester City and being rejected by Lincoln after a few games. But his family immediately settled in Colchester and he never looked back.

Smith summed up Svarc best when he said, 'He has very quick reflexes and is very sharp at taking the half chance when it comes along. He also has a lot of skill.'

Bobby managed only 8 goals in his first season, but was top scorer, with 26 and 25 in following campaigns. His overall U's record was 128 games and 63 goals and one of his best remembered exploits was his four timer against Chester on the old Sealand Road ground.

Later Svarc was joined by former team-mate John Froggatt and the pair forged a wonderful scoring partnership, complementing each other perfectly. I wonder what they think of Boston's recent elevation?

The 1973/74 promotion season was a Smith triumph and their 60 points the highest attained in a League season, beating the 58 of 1956/57. It was a strong division too and U's mixed it for the first time with the likes of Blackburn Rovers, Charlton Athletic and Preston North End. Rovers, now Premiership big boys, finished champions but went under, beaten 2-0 at Layer Road, Jimmy Lindsay and Svarc scoring. Up at Deepdale, U's also won by the same margin.

Bob Jackson recalls that at this game, one of their players met the party off the coach to enquire if Stuart Morgan was playing. He was most relieved to hear he was injured but an equally efficient Ray Harford did the job well enough and scored both goals for full measure. Preston finished the season a disappointing ninth and manager Bobby Charlton, one of many top-line players to fail as managers, was sacked.

Harford, a commanding central defender who was a suave man about town later did remarkably well on the managerial merry-go-round, especially at Blackburn. The whole football world mourned when he tragically died in 2003.

The League Cup run of 1974/75 proved the highlight of Smith's stay and it was a little odd that promotion was not achieved again. U's swept aside

Oxford, Southend and Carlisle in the early rounds and the Roots Hall success was especially impressive with an in-form Steve Leslie twice on target. The Carlisle affair was not without incident, however. They were in the First Division at this time and were in trouble with referee Peter Reeves, who needed a police escort after booking Frank Clarke and Bobby Owen. They had challenged a penalty decision, and all eleven players continued the dispute. The spot-kick was despatched by Leslie and clinched a 2-0 victory, Svarc having already scored from a bad back pass, .

It was not, however, a happy night for Stuart Morgan. The lion-hearted Welshman was in the tough Duncan Forbes mould, and had lots of ups and downs at Layer Road. This was one of the lows, for he sustained a broken collarbone. It completed a rough two weeks in which he had been stripped of the captaincy, reprimanded for bad behaviour, and dropped.

Bob Jackson, after the Carlisle exploits, predicted 'If we get drawn at home, we can go all the way to Wembley', and Jim Smith, getting caught up in Colchester's great cup record said, 'The ground does not help First Division teams and I wouldn't like to come here and face Colchester at Layer Road.'

In the fourth round, U's drew another more glamorous First Division outfit in Southampton who, bossed by Lawrie McMenemy, had an array of talent with star names in Mick Channon and Peter Osgood. Two years on, they were to win the FA Cup, beating Manchester United. But on a miserable rain-swept night which kept the gate down to under 10,000, they were held to a goal-less draw in a dour affair that never reached any great heights. For the first time there were hints of crowd trouble when police with dogs had to break up an affray.

Few gave U's a chance in the replay at The Dell – another homely atmospheric ground that is no more. The form book was upset by a Barry Dominey goal and the save of his life by Mike Walker. Ten minutes from the end with U's desperately hanging on, Channon delivered a rocket free-kick from the edge of the penalty box. The ball was just a blur in the night sky and the goal cry was on everyone's lips, but Walker brought off a miraculous one-handed mid-air save. The charismatic Channon, an England international, blinked in disbelief. He is now a high-flying race-horse trainer turning out sleek two-year-olds as prolifically as he scored goals.

Dominey was a highly improbable match winner. A lanky beanpole of a defender, he was a London teenager who had had only a handful of games and after his Dell moment of glory did little else of note, finishing in non-League with Dorchester. His winner that exciting night was delightfully taken when he rose high to head home a Leslie free-kick.

Colchester dominated most of the match and were convinced they had scored earlier when Svarc got in a header from another Leslie free-kick. Paul Bennett crashed the ball against the underside of the bar but U's players were adamant that it was over the line. Jim Smith's comment was, 'Perhaps the referee did us a favour in the long run because we had to keep pushing forward after that.'

Southampton, who were without the suspended Osgood, did plenty of attacking but were constantly denied by an inspired Walker who told reporters later, 'The Channon save was one of the best of my career. Wembley? Why not? People laugh, but they did that when I was in the Watford side that reached the semi-finals four years ago.'

Walker, highly articulate, was invariably at home on the big stage, and after 522 games for U's, turned to management. After his controversial dismissal at Colchester, he bossed Norwich City, taking them into Europe.

The Southampton tie was a real thriller and one of U's best-ever cup victories. The tension got to the press box and I can recall chain-smoking away a near packet of colleague Robin Frost's cigarettes. Of course, the papers went to town. *Mirror Sport* proclaimed, 'Barry Sinks Saints' and my *Colchester Express* match report heading was, 'Saints Alive, What A Glory Night It Was'.

It was Smith's pinnacle of fame at Layer Road. He was a forthright man with whom it was always easy to communicate. The players respected him and he frequently played cards with them on away trips.

I honestly think he believed Colchester could make the two-legged semi-finals after the Southampton triumph, especially when Aston Villa were drawn at home. But as it turned out, Villa, playing at Layer Road for the first time ever, ran out 2-1 winners in a rather anti-climactic affair, the more so because of the disappointing gate of 11,871. It was a pitiful turn-out really, in view of the nearness to the semi-final.

There have been more glamorous Villa sides. The best-known performers were goalkeeper Jim Cumbes, who was also a well-known county cricketer; Bristol-born speedster Ray Graydon; Ian 'Chico' Hamilton, who cost £40,000 from Southend; and Brian Little who had been an England youth international.

Villa, a club soaked in tradition, were fourth in the Second Division at the time and managed by Ron Saunders who had taken Norwich City and Manchester City to successive Wembley finals. His name was destined to be on the trophy yet again, for Villa went on to the final and beat Norwich City 1-0.

Jim Smith and coach Bobby Roberts had been at Villa Park the previous Friday when they drew with Oxford United. He expressed his confidence in the programme price 1op, which included a profile on Steve Leslie who was in his fourth season and, from being a striker, had developed into an immaculate left-sided midfielder.

The match played on Tuesday 3 December 1974 was more or less settled when Alan Little put Villa in front from brother Brian's pass. U's had their moments and Cumbes made one fine save to deny Lindsay, but Villa ground out efficient if unspectacular football and a goal from the quicksilver Graydon on the hour settled it all. Lindsay Smith took over from Harford and laid on a goal for Froggatt, but it was all too late. U's were left to ponder on what might have been. It had been a fine run and the ever-sage Jim Smith said wistfully, 'Perhaps the rewards were too great.'

There was a downside to the season and that came in the FA Cup when little Leatherhead beat U's by a single goal in a strange second-round tie at their tiny Fetcham Grove ground, packed to the hilt by a 3,500 crowd. The non-Leaguers had a volatile, chatty forward, Chris Kelly, known as 'The Lip' who duly celebrated. Leatherhead proved it was no fluke by ousting Brighton and giving Leicester City a fright at Filbert Street. They led by 2-0 before going under 3-2 – and the Lip was finally silenced!

Colchester finished the campaign in eleventh spot, and the ultimate Champions Blackburn later lured Smith to Ewood Park, and he went on to enjoy some action-packed managerial years. At Layer Road, he had a good coach in Roberts, and some top-line players like ex-Watford duo Mick Packer and Jimmy Lindsay prospered.

The Svarc-Froggatt strike duo thrived and Svarc, who later teamed up again with Smith at Ewood, played 129 Colchester games in total, scoring 59 goals. He went for £20,000 but was once valued at £50,000 when Oxford chased him. Froggatt made 184 appearances, and netted 35 times before he left for Port Vale.

Colchester received £9,000 from Blackburn when Smith was pirated away. It seemed scant compensation for one of the club's best-ever managers, and certainly in the light of future seasons, the most successful on the big stage.

He enjoyed his football and was a character with many a cryptic obser-vation. Bob Jackson, who has kept in close touch with him, remembers the celebrations he had with him the night Oxford clinched promotion to the old First Division. They wined and dined at the Oxford Posthouse until 4 a.m. and in the taxi on the way home Jim solemnly said, 'What you have witnessed tonight is the greatest achievement in the history of sport.'

His Colchester era was certainly some achievement.

Ups and Downs

Red Devils in Town

Colchester have twice encountered Manchester United at Layer Road in cup competitions – memorable events whose excitment many other lower division clubs have yet to sample. Initially, under Bobby Roberts, there was a fifth-round FA Cup tie, and later a Football League Cup tie when Cyril Lea was at the helm. Needless to say, the Red Devils won both.

Manchester United in these pre-Ferguson days were not the world-class contenders of today, but any Old Trafford side were formidable and a tremendous draw. When they came to town, there was a furore of local excitement although, oddly enough, the gate on each occasion was under 14,000.

In 1978/79, Roberts' side too had reeled off an impressive run, having beaten Oxford United, Leatherhead (after a replay), Darlington and Newport County, when another replay was needed. It was the exciting fifth round at that, so one could have expected a near full house – but the weather took a hand.

The tie was postponed from the Saturday, and there was still snow about on the Monday night, the outlying roads in a terrible state. The weather affected the attendance, but those present thrilled to a humdinger of a match, and unlucky U's were within touching distance of a lucrative replay in the Theatre of Dreams.

All the drama came late on. It was still deadlocked when, with eight minutes left, there was all but a major upset. Goalkeeper Gary Bailey was left stranded after blocking Steve Foley, and the ball broke loose to striker Trevor Lee. This surely was it, everyone thought, as he lined up his sights and took deliberate aim. The ball zipped past two defenders only for Arthur Albiston to dramatically clear off the line with an outstretched foot.

A replay surely was still on, but in 85 minutes, Micky Thomas curled in a corner, Andy Ritchie got a header, and Brian Greenhoff found the target with a right-foot shot. Roberts had warned that if the lethal striker was given half a chance, it could be fatal. He had scored in every round.

A crestfallen Roberts said, 'It was sickening. I could not have asked more from my lads. They are sitting in my dressing room absolutely gutted.'

Manchester United boss Dave Sexton's comment, 'It's a bit of a tragedy for Colchester. They did enough to take us back for a replay.'

By their narrow win, Manchester United became the first-ever First Division side to win a major game at Layer Road. Their side, which included Lou Macari and Steve Coppell, went on to Wembley, but lost a gripping final, losing to Arsenal 3-2.

The Colchester tie, for which the actual gate was 13,174, was commentated on by the famed Denis Law, for a northern radio station, and another notable was Jeff Powell, now one of the top sports columnists of the day. Reporting for the *Daily Mail* he said, 'Colchester resisted as stubbornly as the ancient Britons, and were so close to another upset that manager Roberts is unlikely to suffer the same fate as Boadicea in defeat.'

Trevor Lee had one of his best matches, rising to the big occasion. He was Colchester's first famous black player – a lithe classy performer who scored his fair share of goals. Signed from Millwall, he was eventually sold to Gillingham for £90,000, and that, for a long time, was a club record.

Manchester United's second visit was on Tuesday 8 November 1983, and Cyril Lea was then manager. His opposite number was the bluff Ron Atkinson and only Bailey, Albiston and Marcari remained from the 1979 squad. The match was a League Cup tie, then the sponsored Milk Cup, and Manchester creamed their way to a comfortable 2-0 victory.

There were several new faces in the U's line up – Steve Wignall and Stewart Houston, ex-Ipswich Cup final winning hero Roger Osborne and red-haired striker Tony Adcock.

On the night before a 13,031 crowd, class shone through, although U's had their moments early on and that all-purpose defender Gordon McQueen was the key figure in both penalty areas. First he headed off the line, after an Osborne cross had skimmed from the head of non-contract player Dave Hubbick.

Then a minute later, McQueen was at the other end to head the opening goal from a corner by Arthur Graham. That was an early turning point and before half-time it had all been settled with a classic second goal. The mighty Bryan Robson, strutting his stuff brilliantly, laid on a superb pass down the middle and Remi Moses twinkled his way past Wignall to slot the ball past Alec Chamberlain.

The rest was academic and, although Colchester had plenty of the play, they couldn't manage a consolation, although Micky Cook was unlucky a couple of times. On this occasion, Manchester United did not get to Wembley. That was a Merseyside derby won by Liverpool.

Back to Bobby Roberts, who took over the managerial reigns from Jim Smith in 1975. He was a softly spoken Scot whom I seldom heard utter a harsh word. He had an illustrious fifteen-year playing career starting with Motherwell and then coming south to join First Division Leicester City for whom he starred in the 1969 cup final when they lost to Manchester City.

Bobby, a stylish defender, played with and against the greats of his day and first teamed up with U's as a coach – an area where he excelled. He was a good judge of a player and two highly successful signings were strikers Bobby Gough, from Southport, and Colin Garwood, from Huddersfield. Gough, a tough little battler, was a little reminiscent of Bobby Svarc, while Garwood was a more flashy character and a real crowd pleaser.

Both figured in two more well-remembered cup ties. Not too much excitement had been generated since Leeds, but the much-vaunted Derby County came to town in 1977, the game a fifth-round FA Cup tie at that, and United were due some cup success. The previous season, Roberts had smarted after a 4-1 replay humiliation defeat at Dover. Now he faced a side valued at £1.3 million. They were managed by Colin Murphy who had succeeded Dave Mackay and the big name was dazzling Welsh international Leighton Phillips, a player in the £300,000 bracket.

Shrewd tactician Roberts had a game plan. He had watched Derby twice and went on record, 'They will, for sure, make two or three mistakes against us. We have to help them make those mistakes by playing at an unaccustomed pace for them.'

Roberts felt he had assembled the best Colchester side since he arrived, and chairman Jack Rippingale was equally optimistic, 'We have been playing some of the most attractive football seen at Layer Road for several seasons,' he stated.

Jack was one of a long line of chairmen for whom I had the greatest respect. They also included butcher Bill Allen, big Roy Chapman, Bob Jackson, bluff Maurice Cadman and Gordon Parker. All were highly successful in the realms of business, and all devoted so much time to Colchester United. Current chairman Peter Heard maintains the high tradition.

The Derby match created a lot of publicity and there were shades of Leeds when the players were photographed eating oysters. Dick Graham and Ray Crawford both predicted a Colchester win. The *Evening Gazette* put the focus on the wives and girlfriends. I never realised they were such a bevy of beauty and charm. The *Gazette* pictured them in team photo-graph style and they included: Jean Roberts, Connie Williams, Carole Garwood, Wendy Cook, Gladys Froggatt, Mary Packer, Christine Bunkell and Jackie Walker. Also featured was the delightful Betty Scott, the club's first ever woman secretary. Betty was a lovely lady who combined a wonderful personality with high efficiency, something later secretaries, Dee Elwood and the current Marie Partner also accomplished.

Back to the Derby business. Little Gough announced he had a score to settle with Derby defender Colin Todd. Thirteen years earlier, they had met in an English Schools Cup final, Gough playing for Erdington and District and Todd for Chester-le-Street. Gough, who was twenty-seven, cost £7,000 from Southport. He was a lively forward who worried and harried defences. Todd, by contrast, was a £300,000-rated international and one of many Derby big names, others including Kevin Hector, £225,000 David Nish, Charlie George, and ex-Arsenal striker Derek Hales, who cost £300,000 from Charlton.

The tie on Saturday 29 January 1977 attracted a 14,035 crowd and was an exciting but ill-tempered affair on and off the pitch. Hales opened the scoring and, for all their attacking and a string of near misses, it looked as though U's were heading out until a gleeful Garwood came up with a dramatic injury-time equaliser.

There were unseemly scenes in the tunnel at the end and the dressing room windows were smashed. Leighton James complained, 'I have never been kicked so much', but on an incident involving Garwood, he said, 'There was no police involvement. Garwood was just full of himself as you would expect him to be after scoring a vital goal.'

The midweek replay at the now-demolished Baseball Ground was happily less controversial, but a dour slog for all that. Leighton James, who reckoned he suffered a series of insults at Layer Road, had the last laugh for he fittingly scored the winner just before half-time. He made a dazzling run which ended with him hitting a post, and snaffling up the rebound.

Missing the injured Archie Gemmill and George, Derby were made to fight in the second half and U's unlucky moment came when Gough looked all set to equalise but his shot rebounded out off a post and Leslie put the rebound over. Overall, U's were more than a little unlucky not to force extra time and earned the plaudits of a 22,105 crowd.

Roberts managed the team between 1975 and 1982 and a lot of the time his right-hand man was the sleek Ray Harford who later made it in top-line management, chiefly with Blackburn Rovers. Roberts himself had a fair measure of success and picked up two Manager of the Month awards.

The squad opposing Derby were a pretty impressive bunch. In front of him, Mike Walker had Micky Cook, the last remaining member of the squad that encountered Leeds, and John Williams, the former long-serving Watford full-back who had starred with Walker in a 1969/70 cup semi-final. Mick Packer was another former Watford man and Steve Dowman, then a promising eighteen-year-old, was making his mark, as was fleet-footed winger Ian Allinson, then only eighteen, who always had an eye for goals.

Roberts' era threw up the odd high-profile game and there was one cracking 4-0 League Cup win over Jim Smith's Blackburn Rovers. This led to a Leeds United rematch. This time, it was at Elland Road and, with a most clinical display, Leeds won 4-0. Roberts was eventually sacked in Easter 1982, and the fans had a lot of sympathy. He had been sound and honest,but maybe just not hard enough. Certainly he never had much luck.

Following Roberts, there was the short-lived stay of a disillusioned Alan Hunter, and then another ex-Ipswich man in Cyril Lea. He came from

Humberside and had Stewart Houston as coach. One of the top events of this era was the emergence of Perry Groves, a lightning-fast winger. His uncle was former Arsenal ace Vic Groves and young Groves, nicknamed Champagne Perry, emulated his relative by also starring at Highbury among the big lights.

Lee and Houston finally parted company with the club when one Jonathan Crisp threw his hat and chequebook into the arena and the club moved into the most controversial era of all.

Musical Chairs

The Jonathan Crisp saga was the most turbulent period in Colchester United history. Little could Maurice Cadman have realised the strife that would follow his introduction of the self-made-millionaire in 1985.

Crisp was thirty-nine years old and his father a well-known South African Test cricketer. He purchased £75,000 of the club's shares and it was a takeover that was considered timely, for bankruptcy loomed with the club reported to be £140,000 in the red.

A slick-talking dogmatic character who wanted to do things his way, Crisp had long-fancied the idea of owning a League football club. He knew a lot of well-known players and high-profile people in the game and spoke expansively, promising Second Division football in five years.

It all started rosily enough. Crisp, after sacking Cyril Lea and Stewart Houston, had appointed the urbane Mike Walker as manager. Soon United were second in the table and Walker had picked up a Manager of the Month award.

Out of the blue one fateful Sunday after a match at Burnham to mark the opening of their new ground, Walker was summoned by Crisp to a meeting. He went along happily enough believing he was to be offered a new contract. It came as a bombshell then that Crisp insisted Walker and his coach Alan Hunter either resigned or would be sacked. Crisp said they had resigned as a matter of principle and added, 'I have been looking for someone who will want to win for Colchester as much as I have for someone who will be tough and set the right standards.'

Whatever Crisp's ideas of Walker's management, the former goalkeeper went on to great things when boss of Norwich City, taking them into Europe. He was later in charge of Everton for a short spell.

The choice for next manager, after Steve Foley had been caretaker for one match, caused more uprising of eyebrows. Roger Brown had been an virtually unknown defender with Fulham and Bournemouth and had managed Poole Town. Blond and honest enough, Brown started well, winning a Player of the Month award and he spoke of taking the club into the Second Division. İt all went sour, however, with poor results and gates well under 2,000. Events came to a head on Saturday 15 October 1988 when U's crashed to their heaviest defeat ever, a calamitous 8-0 hammering away to Leyton Orient. Richard Wilkins was in that side and frankly had some pretty nondescript players around him.

Brown, of course, had to resign, doing so with dignity. For the umpteenth time, it seemed, Foley was caretaker and had a unenviable job. I could never fathom whether this likeable carefree character really wanted to manage. His heart was certainly in the game and he knew soccer inside out. 'Roger and Out' proclaimed the local press headlines and I wrote in the free sheet *Independent*, 'I am sure a manager of experience would have handled things differently. One could never imagine Layer Road football sinking so miserably with a Dick Graham, or Jim Smith at the helm.'

After Brown left, U's went sixteen games without a win and finished third from bottom. Into the next season, the impatient Crisp lost his money hand-over-fist and turned to big guns. Ex-Ipswich Town striker Paul Mariner, who worked for a spell in the Layer Road promotions office, had been a whisper.

It was to Jock Wallace, twice former Glasgow Rangers manager, and Leicester City boss, who Crisp now turned. Now here was a larger than life figure if ever there was. Jock had the reputation of being as tough as nails, a fearsome sergeant major type with commando-style training. I found that when you could break down his thick Scottish accent, however, there was a soft centre – a little like Dick Graham in fact.

Crisp had met Wallace in Spain where he had been living since managing Seville. He had certainly roughed it in the big time, sacked by Rangers to make way for Graeme Souness. He was also in charge of Motherwell and Hearts and took Leicester to the First Division – but they went down again.

Initially, Wallace was successful. His assistant was World Cup hero Alan Ball, who last encountered Colchester in the FA Cup playing and scoring for Everton. Ball was yet another of Crisp's so-called ace cards. He knew numerous top-line personalities and brought in well-known Irish comedian Frank Carson as a director. At least he made pre-match lounge gatherings highly entertaining.

Wallace was brought from what he thought was retirement in Spain. When he arrived, relegation looked a certainty and U's were rock bottom. It was still in the balance on the run in, but a crucial 2-1 win at Darlington sent the North-Easterners down, Colchester winning the last three games on the trot. In the end, they were 8 points clear of doomed Darlington and Wallace was hailed a hero. Jock had certainly instilled some steel into an ailing side.

Ian Allinson, on his second Colchester spell, and Mario Walsh were consistent scorers and a former amateur striker, Alan Warner, was a surprise success. There was even a mini cup run with Sheffield United taken back to Layer Road after a 3-3 draw. But it all proved a false dawn, largely due to Wallace's failing health. There was only one win in the first nine games and when it was at last ended with a 2-0 victory at Southend, a young Martin Grainger scored on his debut.

Wallace eventually had to quit and was made a director. He was, at this point, a very ill man and Crisp was already enduring hate campaigns from disillusioned punters.

He was now effectively in the last-chance saloon, making a final desperate gamblers throw. The ace card he played this time was former Ipswich Town full-back Mick Mills, who had a distinguished international career.

I felt sorry for Mills, who had been managing Stoke City, but frankly found it difficult to carry his playing success into management. He was highly articulate and smartly dressed and his right-hand man was Sammy Chung, another well-known coach.

Under Mills, Colchester won 8, drew 3 and lost 12 of their last 23 games. Had that record been produced in the first half of the season, relegation would have been avoided. It was incredible too that in early March, Colchester were 8 points clear of Wrexham, then rock bottom.

The end actually came in the penultimate match – a 4-0 defeat away to Cambridge United. It was the most depressing of days. The Abbey Stadium is a ground I have always disliked. It is basic and lacks atmosphere and was even more downbeat for this doom-ridden game which was played on a Sunday. It all seemed so unreal as Colchester folded like a pack of cards. Cambridge won with ease and among the scorers was Steve Claridge.

In the *Evening Gazette* Neil Thomas wrote, 'The lacklustre display was sadly typical of so much of their form this season. Errors in defence, powder-puff challenges in midfield and a total lack of penetration up-front tell the tale not only of one defeat but of the whole campaign.'

A dignified Mills took it in his stride. He had the team in a locked dressing room for half an hour and said afterwards, 'I feel we have the nucleus of a good team to do well next season, but now it's a question of adding to it.'

Mills also predicted a big crowd for the finale game at home to Burnley, for romantic and curiosity reasons. 'The programme alone will be a collector's item' he said.

As it turned out, the wake was attended by a mere 2,778. U's scored first through a Trevor Morgan penalty but lost 2-1. Naturally enough, there was not a dry eye in the house for it was goodbye to the League after forty years and it was naturally hard to accept.

Crisp, who had hit rock bottom in the popularity stakes, blamed some of the players for less than 100 per cent effort. He said the team would stay full-time and he predicted a rapid return to the League fold. Fans were less optimistic, and the proposed new stadium was in the offing – yes, even then – and there was talk of possible ground-sharing with Wivenhoe Town, who had enjoyed stupendous success.

Mills ultimately left by mutual consent and Crisp's fifth manager became another ex-Ipswich skipper, Ian Atkins, who came as player-manager. He was thirty-four and turned down four top-flight clubs for Layer Road. Crisp predicted that U's would be the Liverpool of the Conference, but that looked a bleak prospect after a 2-0 opening day defeat at Yeovil.

Atkins was a tough no-nonsense player, who was an inspired leader, and results improved. Roy McDonough was enlisted as Atkins' hench-man, but despite a good run in with three closing wins, promotion was missed by one point, Barnet taking the prize. Their 3-1 win at Underhill and a point from a Layer Road goal-less draw proved vital. So too did U's dropping two points in a 1-1 home draw against Altrincham, who were very much in the hunt. That game drew 6,986, the biggest gate of the season.

Most unfairly, I thought, Crisp said he was not happy with the season and thought it a disgrace that the only full-time Conference outfit had failed to get promotion. He went on record, 'To come second with a fully professional team in a part-time League – I don't regard as doing well. I think not winning that League was a bloody disgrace.'

It was in July 1991 that Crisp finally decided he had enough and he handed over the chairmanship to James Bowdidge, a thirty-year-old Boxted farmer who had been a U's fan since he was twelve years old. His grandfather was a former chairman, Harold Moore. It ended in acrimony and with more than a little bitterness. Crisp, whom it was reckoned had injected more then a million pounds into an ailing club, said 'I would just like to express my contempt for those people who call themselves loyal supporters but go around tearing down the foundations. They wanted Crisp out, well now they have got it.'

Dave Woods in the *Evening Gazette* summed it up perfectly when he said, 'He has just kicked a habit which cost him £1 million. On occasions he was blowing away £10,000 a week. His habit has caused him sleepless nights and saw him suffer abuse from strangers. Crisp was a man with the initials that suggested he was going to be the U's saviour. Many fans will claim he was in fact a devil in disguise.'

Crisp himself added, 'I wished I had never heard of Colchester United. I should have got out much earlier but the worse it gets, the more determined I get.' He had much more to say about his desire to keep the club going and his final words were, 'I can go to bed and sleep knowing I have given everything my best shot.'

Bowdidge declared that he would launch a shares scheme to give the football club a wider ownership and added, 'We are really giving the club back to the people.' So ended the most controversial period of Colchester United's history. Atkins departed to manage several ailing clubs and is still doing so. And big McDonough bowed in. Thanks to his leadership, U's were soon up and running again.

Gung-Ho Mac

Following Ian Atkins' departure to Birmingham, it was Roy McDonough who proved to be Colchester's saviour and I still say today that the club owes him a huge debt of gratitude. Big Roy, a striker of many clubs, came from Southend for his second and most decisive Layer Road spell. He had a poor disciplinary record and was a rough diamond of a character. But I liked his gung-ho up and at 'em style and he superbly engineered the tremendous 1991/92 double and the return to the League fold.

It was no mean feat and I doubt that managers with better credentials would have fared better. Roy, a real Brummie with accent to match, proved just the right man for a difficult job. Without him, U's might have been stuck in the non-League wilderness for years. The Conference is not the easiest competition to win, even when operating full-time.

His dossier of clubs – they included Chelsea, Exeter, Southend, Walsall and all points east and west – provided Roy with rich experience and he proved very much a player's manager. Several very good performers blossomed under him as U's swept all before them. Readily coming to mind are Mark Kinsella, now a fully fledged Irish international on the world stage, Steve McGavin of the silky skills, and rugged Martin Grainger. Steve didn't quite make the top stage with Birmingham but Grainger certainly did so and became a key figure and free-kick specialist. At his zenith, he was in the £1 million bracket and Colchester grossly undervalued him for £30,000 when he went to Brentford.

Wycombe Wanderers, then managed by Martin O'Neill, were U's main rivals and, in the exciting finale, pipped them on goal difference. The double Colchester achieved, 2-1 winners at Adams Park and 3-0 victors at Layer Road. At Wycombe, goalkeeper Scott Barrett scored the extraordinary winner, a real curio of a goal.

I recall McDonough when the coach arrived at Adams Park, leading the players off with the rallying cry of 'Let battle commence'. One had a mental picture of captain Roy and his men armed to the teeth. He would have been a cartoonist's dream – he and the sleek O'Neill were complete opposites. Games against Wycombe were really something special, and the teams so dominated that third-placed Kettering finished as many as 21 points behind United.

United lost only four games and the one team to win at Layer Road was Farnborough. In the FA Trophy, Kingstonian were close when U's just scraped a 2-2 draw and replay and the Merthyr tie also required a replay. The great Kingstonian escape was remarkable, for Tony English desperately saved the day with a goal two minutes into injury time. In the Bob Lord Trophy, Wycombe gained some sort of revenge by winning 6-2 at Layer Road, but Colchester had won the games that really mattered.

In an action-packed season, the fans gradually came back, and the final home games with the title still at stake saw 6,303 people for the 3-1 win over Kettering, and 7,183 for the 5-0 drubbing of Barrow. Then came the pilgrimage to Wembley for the FA Trophy against Witton Albion. There was a 27,806 crowd for Colchester's first-ever Wembley appearance. You couldn't call it a classic game but McDonough and his troops gave a competent winning performance against the Cheshire side who had knocked them out a year earlier.

Mike Masters, the quiet American and a lethal striker, opened the scoring inside five minutes with a classic header after a throw-in by the versatile Paul Roberts. Then Nicky Smith, on the twentieth minute mark raced in to convert a low Kinsella cross after the sleekest of moves that matched the immaculate turf.

U's were on their way but the game developed into ill-tempered brawl. McDonough and McGavin were booked and three Witton men were also carded. Witton had a glimmer of hope when Mike Lutkevitch headed home and Barrett had to make some timely saves. The ill-feeling boiled up nine minutes from the end when little Jason Cook was sent off for aiming a punch in a flare-up involving several players, but U's response was to seal it when McGavin gleefully caught the opposition napping in swift breakaway.

Eamonn Collins who didn't play but was in the squad, made the splendid gesture of giving the crestfallen Cook his medal. Eamonn, a puck-faced inside forward and a real broth of a boy was a skilful operator who came from Portsmouth and was a former Eire international. He brought back memories of Sammy McLeod and played 96 games in all before moving to Exeter.

Masters, the 6ft-plus Yank, cherished hopes of playing in the World Cup. He was a lethal finisher and scored a memorable hat-trick in the finale win over Barrow, walking off with the match ball. Masters, who had been recommended by ex-Ipswich striker Paul Mariner, ignited the crowd in this crucial match with an explosive twenty-five-yard volley. Masters was a genial character. He was keen to play for U's in the Football League but encountered work permit problems.

Martin O'Neill was bitterly disappointed over missing out on the Conference title – the margin was narrow and Wanderers, like Colchester, had collected a remarkable 94 points. Their last-match win 4-0 against Witton was not enough, but they felt aggrieved, reckoning they were better suited to League football from ground and financial reasons. A local reporter at the last game summed it up well when he said, 'I have never known a 4-0 victory seem so much like a defeat.'

There was always great rivalry between the two clubs, and it still exists today. Wycombe eventually made their mark, O'Neill too. He said, 'At this moment, I have to say I couldn't possibly face another season in the Conference. I want to manage in the First Division and I think I could do it.' He did manage it, taking charge of Leicester City and then really scaling the heights managing Glasgow Celtic. He is also a notable TV soccer pundit.

Colchester's unique double season featured all sorts of records. It was a fun-packed happy era — they usually are when you are winning. There were only four defeats, only one at home and no Conference side had lost fewer games. The best U's season, in fact, since the club was formed in 1937. A sequence of seventeen home wins was a club record and popular keeper Barrett effectively kept the door shut with twenty-nine clean sheets. Layer Road was a fortress again.

The goal glut was led by the doughty McDonough himself with 29 overall. McGavin had 26 and little Gary Bennett, who had spent his early years at White Hart Lane, had a haul of 16. Often underrated, Gary never quite made it at League level but just couldn't stop scoring on the non-League circuit, and later smashed all-time Braintree goal records.

When Player of the Year time came around, popular winger Smith scooped four trophies. Skipper Tony English, honest and dependable and never giving less than 100 per cent, and Barrett also picked up awards. There were so many claimants that wonderful season that the club was firmly placed on the map again.

Roberts, a much-travelled player around the lower divisions, was a versatile defender and McDonough's henchman. A streetwise Benny Fenton type with the gift of the gab, he would often turn up at the ground with cut-price bargain offerings. A great character. At the end of the day, McDonough must take most credit for arguably U's best-ever season. He did it with style and roguish charm and I well remember how expertly he dealt with press and television interviews when the double was achieved, emulating Wealdstone's feat of 1985.

Big Roy goes down as one of the Layer Road legends. In all, after his two League spells and two Conference campaigns, he played 213 games and bagged 62 goals. His leadership continued for a while with the League return before he was sacked – by his club chairman, father-in-law Gordon Parker. So in no way could there be accusations of nepotism!

McDonough's sacking was a good press story, the more so that his wife Jackie was promotions manager of the club. She revealed that they had just sold their house in Whaley Road and said, 'He is out of a home and a job. We are moving in with my mother and father and we can be a family again.'

Parker held a press conference and told the media, 'This is not the most pleasant of days or the most pleasant of tasks. The board felt it would probably be best if a more experienced man was the manager. The decision was taken to cancel the manager's existing contract.' He also pointed that the board's decision had come from a lack of success on the field in recent games and 'a flirtation' with relegation. It was an extraordinary statement and Parker further said of his son-in-law, 'In terms of football management Roy was an inexperienced manager.' In this respect, Parker was probably right. Roy did a superlative job in the double season which was one of the most enjoyable of campaigns, but in the League, he found it harder going. There was also his topsy-turvy domestic life, and the widely read outlandish revelations of personal events in a popular tabloid newspaper which brought about more than a few upraised eyebrows. For all that, however, I always had a soft spot for Roy and his extrovert enthusiasm both on and off the pitch. He was a disarming character who, if he had not opted for soccer, could probably have been an extra in a movie – a bandanna-adorned Mexican bandit comes readily to mind.

The Three W's

Steve Wignall and Steve Whitton were essentially player-managers – clean-cut, tracksuited and highly professional. The man who came between them, Mick Wadsworth, was very professional too, but maybe best described as an enigma.

Wignall, who shone with U's as a dedicated central defender with 336 first-team appearances, was appointed in January 1995 after the George Burley walkout and the caretaker man, Dale Roberts, had had a short spell.

Wiggy, as he was universally known, was Liverpool-born and his other League club was Doncaster Rovers. He sampled the taste of management with Ryman Leaguers Aldershot Town, and it's interesting to recall that TV pundit Mark Lawrenson was among the many other candidates.

Wignall as a manager was unruffled, and one of the rare true gentlemen of the game. I never heard him utter a foul word and when it comes to achievement, he emerges near the top in the list of most successful Colchester men in charge, for he was to oversee two Wembley appearances, another near-miss play-off shot and, of course, promotion.

The play-off disappointment came in 1996, but what a feast of excitement the finale produced. U's just sneaked their big chance with a last match 1-0 win over Doncaster Rovers at Layer Road. The winner was a remarkable goal from former Diss amateur Paul Gibb. He saw his sliced cross from yards out turn out to be an unstoppable shot. Other results went Colchester's way and they just made seventh spot.

It turned out to be Plymouth Argyle in the semi-finals and the first tie at Layer Road – the gate was 6,511 – was a roller-coaster thriller ultimately decided by a picture-book goal by Mark Kinsella, just before half-time. Kinsella, then twenty-three years old, was in his seventh season at Layer Road and he rated his goal as one of the best he had ever scored. Plymouth were a high-priced outfit and it was a remarkable fact that the entire U's squad cost one-third the price of Argyle sub Carlo Corazzin.

Peter Cawley, that rugged no-nonsense defender, was Man of the Match. He had been one of the Wimbledon crazy gang, a giant of a man, but off the field was a good-humoured character with a heart of gold. Wignall assembled an impressive team that included sprightly Chris Fry, Tony McCarthy, Scott McGleish in his first Layer Road spell and fellow striker Robbie Reinelt.

Robbie was a slick scorer who I always thought should have done better. He has been a prolific marksman wherever he has played and reaped a rich harvest of goals with Braintree in the Ryman League.

U's fancied their chances of Wembley and the second leg at Home Park was a bad-tempered business when Plymouth boss, Neil Warnock, became the centre of controversy, and not for the first time. The feisty Warnock was banned from the touchline and he riled Colchester by saying they had no right to be there alongside his Plymouth team.

Warnock had also stirred things up with comments about the Colchester crowd intimidating his players at Layer Road. He said, 'One of the lads said he got hit by an apple and others said coins were thrown on the pitch. Let us hope our supporters are just as hostile.' It was a close-run thing at Home Park with U's heartbroken to go down 3-1, although another Kinsella strike gave them hope as an away goal decider for a short spell. Plymouth went on to beat Darlington for the big prize, but they never stabilised, and dropped down again.

The disappointment of 1996 was soon forgotten and, inside a year, Colchester were at Wembley in the Auto Windscreen final. This satellite competition of so many sponsors has its critics, but the final stages can throw up money-spinners and if you made Wembley, a great family fun day beckoned. So it was with U's who, in the final, met Carlisle, then quite a force. It was reckoned that around 20,000 Colchester fans made the journey although they were outnumbered as Carlisle had an estimated 25,000 followers. The official attendance was 45,077 people.

Just as for the FA Trophy, Colchester's blue and white army whooped it up down Wembley Way and there was a great atmosphere as they indulged in good-humoured banter with their Cumberland rivals. Not one serious incident was reported. Wembley was becoming obsolete for sure, but I'm convinced that traditionalists are already missing the famous towers.

To reach Wembley, Colchester had to beat old rivals Peterborough in a semi-final second leg and the hero of the hour was Paul Abrahams, the sprightly striker who had been sold to Brentford for £45,000. Wignall brought off a coup by buying him back for £20,000. Abrahams never settled at Griffin Park. He was skilful, pacy and a goal-grabber who came up through the youth ranks. This likeable lad and former Gilberd School pupil, I always believe, lacked a little in self-belief and under-achieved. He is still operating in the Ryman League.

It was certainly a match to remember. Posh arrived with boss Barry Fry and owned a two goal first-leg advantage, but Paul Buckle and Chris Fry levelled it up for a sudden-death affair to be settled by a golden goal. Abrahams decided it in the 100th minute with a fantastic swerving shot from twenty-five yards that left keeper Bart Griemink clawing air. Abrahams, who had expected to be on the bench said, 'That was the best night of my life' and of the golden goal enthused, 'I caught it well but lost it until I saw the net ripple.'

Young Paul provided a funny story. He had vowed to run straight down the pitch and down to the pub if he scored but, as he said, 'Almost straight away I was deluged by supporters. It was fantastic.' That fabulous character

Fry, as ever magnanimous in defeat, wished Colchester good luck and, of the winning goal, he cryptically observed, 'The 'keeper hadn't a clue and I doubt if the scorer had either.'

That night was a great one too for the Gregory brothers. David featured in the U's win and brother Neil, later to join Colchester for £50,000, shot Ipswich Town into the play-offs with a hat-trick in the 3-1 win over Sheffield United.

Back to the final. It was on Sunday 20 April 1996 and, after a gruelling deadlocked game full of near-misses, it all came down to a penalty shoot-out. Colchester have a poor record in this controversial area. So it proved again as, heartbreakingly, they lost 4-3. The most crestfallen player was Karl Duguid, then an unknown fledging. Colchester led 3-1, but Duguid missed, so too did Peter Cawley and U's were beaten – it was all so nail-biting for the breathless crowd. Skipper Richard Wilkins, Tony Adcock and David Greene scored from the spot. Paul Conway, Dean Walling, Warren Aspinall and Steve Hayward were the Carlisle marksman. Carl Emberson had brilliantly saved from Owen Archdeacon and Carlisle 'keeper Tony Caig admitted to cheating by moving before the kicks were taken.

Afterwards, Duguid was inconsolable, but as Derek Davis in the *Evening Gazette* wrote, 'Duguid should not hold his head in shame. He should stand proud that he was prepared to be one of five volunteers to go for goal. More senior pros who did not step forward should look in the mirror and ask themselves questions'. The game in normal and extra time had been dour with unrelenting chances at both ends – the best of the U's being seconds from the end. Sale set up Joe Dunne who closed in only to shoot over. Dunne said, 'My legs were cream-crackered but that's no excuse. If I had scored young Dugi wouldn't have missed his penalty – in fact the game wouldn't have gone to penalties at all.'

A crestfallen Duguid bemoaned, 'I shed more than a tear or two because I was so confident I was going to score. It wasn't a bad penalty as spot-kicks go. The keeper got a great touch and it was enough to put the ball onto the post.'

Steve Whitton, then assistant manager and aged thirty-six said, 'I thought my chances of playing at Wembley had gone. It was a great feeling and I've got to try and remember that.' The disappointments were soon a thing of the past for the following season was Wembley all over again.

Colchester, in fact, only missed automatic promotion by one point. They disposed of Barnet in the semi-finals and it was Torquay United in the final.

Wignall had assembled a very good squad and it was a wonder season for David Gregory, the all-purpose midfielder who simply couldn't stop scoring. He finished as leading marksman with 11, many of them from the penalty spot. Big Mark Sale was next with 8. He was a tall striker over whom fans seemed divided. It appeared a question as to needing a tall target man or a more mobile striker wanting the ball on the ground, but Sale, a man of the world character who liked a bet and who had constantly moved around the lower division circuit was impressive on his day.

The final was the least exciting of Colchester's three Wembley visits. It was settled by a Gregory penalty in the twenty-second minute after Jon Gittens had handled a Sale header. The match was played on a Friday night and undoubtedly affected the attendance, which was a disappointing 19,486. Colchester deservedly triumphed and were the better side by far. Simon Betts was a whisker away from scoring and there should have been a second penalty when ex-U's man Paul Gibbs hacked down Gregory. Richard Wilkins, who had been named Player of the Year, took the trophy and it was Steve Wignall's proudest moment – he had taken Colchester into Division Two for the first time.

But things turned sour the next season when U's suffered their most humiliating FA Cup defeat ever, crashing 4-1 to unknown north-eastern non-Leaguers Bedlington Terriers. It was like losing to the likes of Braintree or Heybridge Swifts and undoubtedly this humiliating event and a lack of cash to strengthen led to Wignall's surprising decision to quit. He announced, 'I've taken the club as far as I can' and he did not elaborate.

Steve Whitton had expected to take over but, in their wisdom, the board controversially went for Mick Wadsworth, then forty-eight, a man who had rocky spells with Carlisle and Scarborough. The directors were obviously beguiled by his coaching talent – he had been a backroom boy in Bobby Robson's 1990 World Cup squad.

But Wadsworth, a dogmatic personality with whom it was often diffi-cult to communicate, was not especially popular. He made dubious sign-ings and had a shock clear-out of established favourites. Neither did the fact that he conducted some of the club affairs from his home in the North help endear him to the fans.

Of his new recruits, Jamie Moralee, a much-travelled striker who had been right out of form, was arguably the biggest flop. Another, Irishman Brian Launders, cost the club a lot of money in lengthy legal wrangling over his contract, but credit where credit is due, Wadsworth did have some successes. I liked loan-striker Bradley Allen who went to Grimsby where he scored prolifically. Simon Brown, Joe Keith and Thomas Pinault too settled in and became key squad members. Another Wadsworth player at Layer Road, defender Efe Sodje, is now with Huddersfield and was on the World Cup 2002 stage as a Nigerian international and played in the England match.

Wadsworth was nothing if not an innovative manager and always looked to pull a prize rabbit out of the hat. He thought he had done so when he played Brazilian Jose Antunes in the big Manchester City clash at Layer Road. Jose was reputed to be a new star on the horizon but it was case of 'now you see him, now you don't' for he lasted just fourteen minutes before being knocked out and carried off after a collision. He vanished from Essex, signed for Barnsley and then disappeared from the scene.

There were up and down results and rumblings of discontent and, after the shock resignation of managing director Stephen Gage, the unsettled Wadsworth quit, something which frankly pleased most of the soccer public. He eventually went North first as Bobby Robson's right-hand man at Newcastle and then as Oldham Athletic boss, with a brief spell at Southampton in between. Since then, he has moved again, taking over Huddersfield on the recommendation of Sir Bobby, but his McAlpine Stadium reign ended when he quit towards the end of season 2002/03. Most recently he guided the DR Congo to three defeats in the 2004 African Cup of Nations.

Next came Steve Whitton who had waited patiently for his big managerial chance. Popular Steve has an exemplary playing career with his chief clubs, Birmingham, West Ham and Ipswich, and as boss he ran a good ship. He proved a good tactician, a believer in the passing game and with limited resources, competed well in a division where standards are high and where there is much mega-money. He had his critics and his team selections were sometimes puzzling, but I like the man and I liked his style.

Momentarily at the start, after a wondrous 6–3 opening-day win at Chesterfield, U's were in the top three. But frankly, survival was the name of the game and between them, Wignall and Whitton ensured stability with U's very much part of the new twenty-first century game.

I was personally saddened when Whitton eventually parted company with the club and Phil Parkinson breezed in with immediate success to start a new era. Under Parky, a new adventurous spirit has sprung up and we have a quality squad. There is a more positive approach with strikers galore.

Since then, Wignall won his way back into managership landing but then losing the Southend United job in six hectic months. I would personally love to see Whitton back on the circuit. He has much to give to the game. So much was achieved at Layer Road under Wignall and Whitton with much prestige restored. Manchester City and Stoke City were met for the first time, and very excitingly, glamorous Fulham and Kevin Keegan came to town before the Cottagers rapid rise to the Premiership. We have also had Colchester's first Third World star and million-plus transfer with Lomana Lua Lua – few players have captivated a Layer Road crowd so dramatically and his blossoming career at Newcastle is avidly followed.

It's extraordinary that at the same time, Colchester's top-priced signings are in the £50,000 bracket, but the board's admirable aim has always been for Colchester to retain its League football, a status in constant doubt with more than one lower division club these suddenly uncertain days.

Then of course there is the much-needed new all-seat multi-purpose stadium. Hopefully it's just around the corner, although there will be a universal sadness when we have to say goodbye to dear old Layer Road.

Local Heroes and the Old Enemy

Vic Keeble

There is no more popular player with the fans than a local-born star who has come up through the ranks. Vic Keeble, who later achieved fame with Newcastle and West Ham, is such a U's legend. Were he playing today, one could add fortune to fame for Vic would surely be a top-money earner in the Premiership.

Keeble was a goalscoring centre forward. He started out with the King George V club and when he went to Colchester Royal Grammar School, rugby was the game and Vic excelled in the handling code as he did in many other sports. He was equally good at cricket, table tennis and snooker but soccer kept calling and at seventeen, this boyish-faced gangling lad played his first Colchester United game away to Bedford – and hit a hat-trick in a 5-1 win!

Keeble had to wait a couple of seasons however before he established himself. He had to compete with experienced Arthur Turner for the number nine shirt. The Colchester crowd were invariably split into two camps over the pair, and I fancy even manager Jimmy Allen could never make up his mind as to who was the best. Keeble was the rangy dashing type and brilliant in the air while Turner, a skilled ball and also a good header of the ball, scored readily but often looked slow and cumbersome.

It was 1949/50, U's last Southern League campaign, before Keeble claimed a regular spot. He missed only one match that memorable season, scoring a phenomenal 45 goals and the big clubs were beginning to take note. The starry-eyed lad was highly popular and there were few more exciting sights than Keeble haring for goal or coming up with a copybook Tommy Lawton-like header. Vic thoroughly enjoyed his Colchester football and he reflects on how the game has changed. He recalls, 'On a match day we used to have a snack at the Albert Hotel and then walk to the town, often catching a bus to the ground with the supporters.'

Keeble made limited appearances when Colchester broke into the Football League – he was still competing with Turner – but he became more of a fixture in 1951/52 and registered brilliant hat-tricks against Plymouth and Bristol City.

Then in January on a snowbound Shrewsbury railway station, Jimmy Allen asked him if he fancied a move and when starry-eyed Vic was told it was Newcastle United that were in for him, he blinked in disbelief. As he reminiscences, 'Three days later there I was in the Charing Cross Hotel with Stan Seymour and two directors signing on for £15,000 – and I got a £10 signing on fee.' It was a momentous move for the young Keeble who was, at this stage, a serviceman. He was a home-loving lad so how would the kid from the sticks fare when he rubbed shoulders with giants of the game like Jackie Milburn and Bobby Mitchell? He recalls, 'Being in the Army, I only saw them on match days. I settled in quickly although playing in front of 60,000 crowds was a little intimidating.' The young Keeble was soon scoring goals – in fact he made it to the fastest 50, a Newcastle record until Andy Cole surpassed the feat.

Keeble muses on how the game had changed. Mainly it's the difference in the ball, the footwear and the state of pitches, 'After Christmas, they were often an inch or two deep in mud. Now they are like bowling greens,' he says.

Recently they invited Vic back to Newcastle to see them play Manchester City and he was in absolute awe of the new stadium. The occasion marked the FA Cup final of 1954/55 when Newcastle won 3-1. Keeble played inside right to Milburn, and although he didn't score, he brought German-born Bert Trautmann to one brilliant save. The final and his cup-winners medal are Vic's most treasured memories. On the final,

Vic reminisces, 'When we got a first-minute corner, I went to the back post and Milburn to the front. Three City defenders went with me but no-one went with Jack and there he was scoring with a header when even Jack admitted he couldn't head a ball for toffee. It was almost like cheating.'

Vic adds that the team stayed south on the Sunday before returning triumphantly to Tyneside on the Monday. He recalls, 'There were crowds waiting at all the stations on the way home cheering us and wanting to see the Cup. Finally at Newcastle there were thousands on the streets. That 1955 team was a very special Newcastle team and I was proud to be part of it.' At St James' Park, Vic's all-time record was 69 goals in 121 appearances, well over a goal every other game.

In an interesting story over his cup-winners medal, Vic is said to have been offered £5,000 for it, but he didn't sell. He says however, 'It did get me thinking what the medal might be worth. It's just there in the drawer. The money would be useful, and I wonder whether I should sell.'

Newcastle went close to Wembley too in 1955/56, reaching the sixth round before losing 2-0 to Sunderland. Earlier they pipped Fulham 5-4 at Craven Cottage. Vic scored twice in this thriller and one of them came when he charged goalkeeper Ian Black, ball and all, over the line. You wouldn't see anything like that today.

In 1957, Vic moved south. West Ham paid £10,000 for him and again the signing on fee was £10. At the time, the Hammers, managed by Ted Fenton, were fourth from bottom, but Keeble, on target on his debut in a 1-1 draw against Doncaster, sparked off an amazing run. The team lost only three times in thirty games and finished Second Division champions by one point from Blackburn Rovers.

I well remember the move Vic made south. All the time, his wife Joan, who had just had a baby daughter, had been living in Colchester. The domestic situation and the fact that he often played second fiddle to Milburn led to his discontent. Oddly enough, there were whispers that he might rejoin Colchester and after he retired, some people were even championing him for the managers job. Vic was that sort of folklore legend.

If you reflect today, the mind boggles as to what Keeble could have achieved with the modern plastic footballs. He was an absolute marvel with the old ones and they used to jest at St James' that he could take a penalty with his head! I would have loved to see him in today's Premiership. I reckon he would have been a sensation.

Keeble was the toast of the Boleyn Ground and struck up a splendid scoring partnership with John Dick, a gangling Scottish lad who made his mark with Crittall Athletic – now Braintree Town. He was a shy unassuming lad and, in 1959, won a Scottish cap. Between them, Keeble and Dick scored 50 goals and West Ham were in the top flight for the first time in twenty-six years.

Keeble continued to score prolifically, but a bad back injury brought his career to a premature end. In fact he was only twenty-nine when he had to call it a day. I met up with him again when he joined the *Colchester Express* for whom he wrote a weekly column and worked in the circulation department. He remained as always a cheery character despite suffering a lot of pain which necessitated him lying on his back for long periods of time. The injury was not a soccer one. It was a prolapsed disc and he picked it up playing badminton in the gym – as has been said, Vic was a dab hand at many sports.

Later Keeble successfully ran Colchester United fundraising competitions and did the same for Chelmsford City, finally becoming secretary of the then Southern League club. Today he rarely watches soccer. He pays the occasional visit to Ipswich and, of course, had closely followed the fortunes of Chris, his son from his second marriage whose short career with the U's was impaired by injury. His one League goal was typically a vintage header, right out of his father's top draw.

Keeble must surely muse over the astronomical wages being earned in the Premiership and reflect wryly on his £10 signing on fees. I like to remember him as a boyish-faced coltish striker roared on by patriot U's fans who simply adored him. The game would probably have been one of those epic Southern League local derbies against Chelmsford City on a crisp November Layer Road afternoon with 14,000 crammed in. What a fascinating era.

Peter Wright

It's odd how the early careers of Vic Keeble and Peter Wright were so similar. Wright, the fair-haired outside left who thrilled Layer Road crowds with his dazzling touchline runs and goals, started out at

Colchester Royal Grammar School. Like Keeble, he was soon in the first XV as a promising fly half, and also like Vic, he was an attractive fast-scoring batsman making the school cricket eleven and graduating to Colchester and East Essex and the Young Amateurs of Essex. Three times he topped 1,000 runs.

Teachers and coaches alike predicted a cricketing future so how strange that in early days, younger brother John was reckoned the better foot-baller, but as it turned out, things ended differently. John excelled at the summer game and was one of the big stalwarts of Colchester and East Essex and twice he played for Essex in Championship matches at the Castle Park.

The lure of soccer was irresistible to the ever-ambitious Peter Wright. He was 6ft and very athletic, and playing for Mile End Rovers originally as an inside left, soon attracted attention.

Now as a well-preserved seventy years old, Peter has a twinkle in his eye when he recalls those far-off days which saw Jimmy Allen sign him as a part-timer at £3 a week. There isn't one ex-Colchester player that I know who has nothing but supreme praise for Jimmy Allen. Peter says, 'he was like a father figure and he did so much for me, advising and encouraging.' Incidentally, when Peter signed, Colchester donated £10 to Mile End for playing kit.

In his rambling comfortable Abberton home, Peter browsed through his scrapbooks. He has a remarkable memory of games and opponents. The highlights include his first Colchester game for the 'A' team against Ipswich Town 'A' in the Border League when, due to a player turning up late, he played left-wing for the first time. In his first reserve game against West Ham in the Eastern Counties League, he hit the winner. This was the Football League debut on Saturday 23 March 1953 at Northampton, the same game Kevin McCurley made his bow.

Peter had only just turned eighteen and was given a rough time by a defender called Maurice Canlin. Skipper Reg Stewart took objection and, in the end, dished it out in no uncertain manner to the full-back. He was expecting a rollicking, but enthused manager Jimmy Allen said to him afterwards, 'That's the best thing you have done all day.' It took a while for Wright to make his mark but after what he called a blinder against Bristol Rovers he was more a regular. From 1952 to 1964 he played a total of 448 games and scored 98 goals. Most were with his favoured left foot and many headers, but there were a few with what he called his right foot swinger, notably the winner against Queens Park Rangers at the old White City, one of his highlight games.

Another that jogs the memory was the 1959 FA Cup replay against Yeovil on their dreaded slope. It had been a 1-1 draw at Layer Road but, on a wet skidding top, U's sparkled and won 7-1. It was little short of sensational as Yeovil hadn't been beaten for years on their infamous patch and to win so emphatically was amazing. Wright recalls, 'Everything came off for me and I had one of my best games ever.' Press reports were good and John Camkin of the *News Chronicle* said, 'This lad could well wear an England shirt.'

One of Wright's biggest attributes was his versatility and he revelled in being given a roving commission, popping up on the other flank and often in the middle. He was an expert finisher and could come up with spring-heeled headers. Other big games in the Wright memory scrapbook include the classic Ipswich encounter of 1957 and the Arsenal cup ties two years later. Of the titanic Ipswich clash he reminisces, 'I always did well against Larry Carberry and we murdered them and should have won, especially as Ted Phillips was crocked. It was my benefit, and there was a collection. As a result I bought my first car.' One lost count of the times Wright was about to sign for a leading First Division club. Practically all of them were keen at one time or another but Peter steadfastly stayed put. He had lucrative employment as a draughtsman and his father Ben constantly advised him not to move. Ben was a lovely man, an ex-Army footballer who came down heavily on the side of caution. I recall his words, 'I have seen too many players thrown on the scrapheap after injury with no trade to turn to.'

Daily Herald scribe Peter Lorenzo once wrote that Wright was the most wanted winger in Britain and Peter does have some regrets. He always fancied Wolves, his boyhood dream club and at one point it did seem he was set for Birmingham. Peter had asked for £1,000 cash and was going to St Andrews accompanied by Fenton when the deal was called off.

As a lower division player, Wright reaped untold success and popularity. The Colchester fans adored him and more often than not he had the world at his feet. He played for Third Division South *v.* North, he was the first player to wear contact lenses and the first Third Division performer to score under floodlights at Reading's old Elm Park. He also scored twice against the great Gordon Banks who was making his League debut with Chesterfield. On the wall in Peter's house is a framed action photograph of the match signed by the 'keeper – one of the all-time greats.

There are many interesting stories of Peter's contact lenses – he once lost them during a game – and his eyesight failings were the result of a freak accident in his early days of 1950, when he bumped into a lamp post. At first it was thought he had fractured his skull and he was so impaired that he failed to make the grade for national service.

I like Peter's views on the changing face of football. He argues, 'It's all relative. I think the game is basically more skilful and certainly faster today. With special diets and sophisticated training they are probably fitter, but those wages are a bit silly and how would they cope with the old leather laced ball especially on a mud heap? Then there were the heavy boots and encumbrances such as hefty shin pads.'

When you talk of managers, Wright has no doubts. Benny Fenton was the best, a great motivator and a splendid attacking wing half. Peter said, 'We had our ups and downs but he helped tremendously.' On the famed Fenton temper, he added, 'He liked his tipple and sometimes let rip after a game when he didn't think a certain player hadn't pulled his weight but it only happened when he was not playing.'

Neil Franklin was one manager with whom Wright did not see eye to eye, and he was blamed as a major reason why Peter didn't emigrate to Australia. Before the end of the season he ventured to say to Neil that he didn't seem to figure in his plans and would he be kept? Franklin said he would have to wait for the retained list. At the end of the day he was released but his interrupted emigration plans were disrupted and it all fell through.

When he did leave Layer Road, Peter had spells with Romford, where he was generously paid; Haverhill Rovers and Halstead Town. His management of Woods Leisure Centre followed and highlights continued to crop up. His son Steve had an interesting soccer career with Colchester, playing 143 games, and then starred in European Cup games for Helsinki. In 2001 came a major personal honour. Peter was voted by *Evening Gazette* readers as Colchester United Man of the Century – a supreme honour.

Peter has continued to live a full life, enjoying golf and bowls and gardening and still has a one-day-a-week part-time job. He is a season ticket holder at Layer Road and is the kindliest of men, liking nothing better than a yarn about his playing years.

I have an indelible memory of him in action – speedy, skilful with a rapier-like finish. In other words, a good old-fashioned winger when wingers were very much in vogue.

Bobby Hunt

Bobby Hunt, one of five brothers, was the Colchester United scoring sensation of the early 1960s. He was tough, fearless, two-footed, good in the air and all in all, the type of courageous striker managers dream about.

In 1960/61 when Benny Fenton's team swept all before them in a Fourth Division promotion triumph, Hunt scored 40 goals, the most ever in a Football League season by a U's player. It was, in fact, reduced to 39, one that was scored against Accrington Stanley being wiped out as Accrington folded and their records were expunged. U's had beaten them twice and were one of the last teams to play at Peel Park when the crowd was only 1,441 and no programmes were printed.

In total, Hunt played 164 U's games and scored 99 goals before embarking on an intriguing career in higher divisions with Northampton Town, Millwall, Ipswich, Charlton and Reading. His best-known brother was Ronnie Hunt, a terrier-like midfielder who tragically died a few years back. Billy, another of the footballing family, played just one Colchester game and Peter was an amateur with Ipswich. Their father was an Army man and all his sons had soccer in the blood.

Bobby, a bouncy, jaunty, almost over-cocky youngster, developed via London Schoolboys and Colchester Reserves. To be a goalscorer was his aim but he always admired wingers Mike Grice and Peter Wright and the manner in which they got to the byline and pulled the ball back.

It was an exciting flair that Hunt was to possess. He was not especially pacy but had that knack of winning byline balls and under severe pressure getting them across from the tightest of angles. He made his debut when sixteen in a home 2-2 draw against York City and scored with a header. He also netted in his first-ever cup tie against Maidenhead. The goals flowed that 1961/62 campaign and Bobby scored in ten successive matches between 23 October and 23 December which must be some sort of record.

He had a most complimentary ally in Martyn King who, while the exact opposite temperament-wise, was the perfect foil. The pair fed off each other and King's tally was 33. At one point he scored in seven consecutive games and the duo reached a high over the Christmas period when each hit a four-timer in the record breaking 9-1 win over Bradford City.

It was extraordinary really because in the game at Valley Parade four days earlier, City had won 4-1. The teams travelled back by train together and Bobby laughingly wondered if the City players had lived it up. Whatever, at Layer Road they were slaughtered, six of the nine coming in the last twenty-five minutes. Bobby can recall a rocket drive, a header and a penalty on an afternoon when Colchester could probably have won with Percy Ames blindfolded. It would have been ten but for Bobby Hill hitting the woodwork.

Speculation was rife that Hunt would be sold to a top-line club and, more than once, Newcastle United were in the hunt. They had a £14,000 bid turned down and Bobby relates now that at the time, Benny Fenton was keen on him going to Spurs. It was a time of high-market rumour and Ronnie Hunt was the subject of Fulham interest.

Newcastle eventually signed Scunthorpe's Barrie Thomas, another consistent goal man for £45,000 but were still keen on Bobby. They were looking to pair up the current highest scorers in the country and Bobby was keen to go and emulate Vic Keeble years earlier. It was not to be, but Colchester duly won promotion and Hunt finished with another four-timer against Doncaster in the last game. What a goal-feast campaign it was, with winger Peter Wright also stacking up 14 goals including a hat-trick.

Bobby Hunt, these days a very fit-looking sixty-year-old, puts that season down as his best ever and looks back with fond memories. He says, 'It was a different game then. We didn't think too much about money, the big thrill was just to wear a Colchester United shirt.'

'Then later, if you were married, a club house was of paramount importance. Today I think we have gone over the top and the money earned is immoral. But you can't really blame the player as it can be a short career.'

Bobby has a fund of stories and is amazed how the game has changed. He still chuckles over the day Martyn King opted for playing in the Colchester Tennis league finals instead of leading U's in a match at

Bournemouth. I too remember it well and the controversy it created. Colchester Casuals striker John Baines played instead, one of only four appearances he made. The King incident was, of course, something that would never happen today.

Then there is the new-styled plastic football with which a player can achieve so much. Bobby reckons his late brother Ronnie, who was a long-throw specialist, would have propelled almost the full width of the pitch. Ronnie was a quality performer and Fulham boss of the time Eddie Lowe once described him as the Dave Mackay of the Fourth Division.

Benny Fenton was a manager who Bobby rated highly, often influencing his career. Neil Franklin was a man he never really got to know for Franklin quickly sold him to Northampton Town for £20,000. The Cobblers were unfashionables and were what you could call the famed snakes and ladder club for they shot up to the First Division in successive seasons and then just as quickly dropped back again to the Fourth.

Bobby mixed it with the elite as when he tangled with Manchester United, who paraded Bobby Charlton, George Best and Denis Law before a packed County Ground – that peculiar cricket-soccer combined venue that is now no more. The game is Bobby's chief scrapbook event. It was a 1-1 draw and he hit the equaliser late on with a thirty-yard volley.

He was only twenty-two at the time and it was a career peak. A move to Millwall followed, linking up again with Benny Fenton but Bobby was not over happy at The Den. There were hints he might come back to Colchester but Ipswich Town was the next stop. The managers there were Bill McGarry and then Bobby Robson.

Not for the first time, Hunt was part of horse-trading. Ipswich had sold Gerry Baker to Coventry for £20,000 and bought Bobby for £12,000. He recalls, 'McGarry was a hard man and Robson great for tactics. Bill wanted me to live in Ipswich but I travelled from Colchester and I was blasted when I arrived late after a car accident. McGarry was so irate he didn't even ask how I was. '

Three years at Portman Road where he competed with Ray Crawford were followed by three at Charlton under Theo Foley and then one at Reading. Hunt could finally boast he played in every division of the Football League with an overall goal tally of 130-plus.

Spells at Maidstone, Bury Town as manager and Colchester United reserves wound up his career and he was promotions manager at Layer

Road for a while. He has no regrets, not even about the catalogue of injuries he ran up — a cracked skull, shoulder injuries, broken wrists and removed cartilages among them — all the legacy of getting in where it really hurts. United have never had a more gutsy striker than Bobby Hunt.

The Ipswich Connection

The rise of Ipswich Town was meteoric storybook stuff. They turned professional in 1936 and inside two years were elected to the Football League. They have never looked back, winning both the First Division championship and the FA Cup.

Europe has also been sampled and their Premiership baptism was sensational. Now the Tractor Boys are a household soccer name with a fabulous stadium to match. You could never have predicted it in 1936 but right from the outset with the backing of the powerful Cobbold family they thrived on and off the pitch. I always suspected they were destined for great things.

Among my soccer memorabilia, I have an Ipswich Town handbook marking their first-ever season. It makes fascinating reading. On the board of directors — chairman J.M. Cobbold — were two Right Honorables, two Sirs, and a Lieutenant Colonel!

A survey of the first season mentions that in July 1936, the Portman Road playing pitch was still encircled with posts and ropes and only four players had been engaged. Yet at the end of August when the ball started rolling in the game against Tunbridge Wells Rangers, a full professional side was fielded. That opening game drew a crowd of 11,577.

Invariably Ipswich were always a step ahead of rivals Colchester United who became professional in 1937, and it has remained the case ever since. Geographically, Ipswich were better placed and could count on considerable support from the large rural areas and towns like Stowmarket, Sudbury and Bury St Edmunds who had amateur clubs. Portman Road too lent itself more readily to development as compared to Layer Road. It was central and close to the mainline station.

The ground expanded rapidly and the first Churchman's stand was then quite a sight. The rest of the ground comprised a low all-seat stand with a foreground standing paddock that ran the entire length of the pitch. Opposite this, the ground was uncovered, but there was covered terracing at the Portman Walk end. Iron railings around the perimeter and a large-sized clock at one corner gave the ground a very professional look.

Crowds and results were instantly encouraging and it was immediate lift off. The average gate in their first season was 8,000 and the Southern League championship was won for full measure.

There was also an FA Cup run starting from the earliest preliminary round, and Third Division Watford were met and beaten before a 15,030 crowd before a shock defeat at home to unknown Spennymoor. When Colchester joined the professional ranks, there was quickly the first ever U's *v.* Ipswich competitive contest and it was a titanic thrill-packed game and occasion. It is difficult to imagine how different Layer Road looked then and one wonders what a traveller going back in time would make of it all. The grandstand was a quarter of its present size and there was some small nondescript covering where the barsiders reside today. The rest of the ground was open with no terracing as such. There were no club offices, the dressing rooms were primitive and the turnstiles wooden and ramshackle.

That was the scene, and how they shoehorned in an 11,000 crowd was a near miracle. I love the story too of the misadventures of the travelling Ipswich team coach. It broke down with clutch trouble just outside Colchester and the players were transported to Layer Road by passing cars and buses. This underlines again the closeness between fans and players in those days.

The match was in September and the weather was glorious when Colchester ran out to a great roar. This was only their third game as professionals. They had lost at Yeovil and beaten Bath City 6-1 at home the previous Thursday. Already professional football after years of mundane amateurism had everyone in a feverish grip. Both teams had well-known soccer names whose league clubs held their registrations. They could play non-League with no transfer fees involved and one of the Ipswich stars was George McCluckie, the Aston Villa and Scotland midfielder. He was balding and thanks to his exuberant approach quickly became a hated figure by the Colchester fans. Certainly in today's arenas he would have collected a stack of cards.

United's big personality was also a Scot – Alec Cheyne, a ball-playing wizard still on Chelsea's books and a prolific scorer. The game began sensationally. After two minutes, ex-Aston Villa winger Jackie Williams had scored and the Town fans were in high glee when Gilbert Alsop made it 2-0 after quarter of an hour. Alsop was a stocky figure, a well-known goal man who had made his name with Walsall featuring in the famed giant-killing team that knocked out Arsenal in 1932. By a rare coincidence, he was opposed by Colchester central defender George Leslie, who had been in the same Walsall side.

After the early shocks, U's settled down and in five gripping minutes leading up to half-time drew level. Little George Crisp fired home a cracker and then full-back Alex Wood equalised via a penalty. Fred Houldsworth pushed his first shot against a post and Wood snapped in the rebound. The second half was cut and thrust and on a knife edge, but it looked as though Colchester had won the day when Cheyne put them in front for the first time from Arthur Pritchard's pass. With ten minutes remaining, Leslie was penalised and George Perrett squared it at 3-3 from another penalty. Again it was rebound conversion after Ronnie Dunn had beaten out the first shot.

The result was about right and the *East Anglian Daily Times* reported, 'The game was full of thrills and shocks and ended with the deserving sharing of points, a result which if not damaging the stock of Ipswich should raise considerably that of the new venture. It should dispel from the minds of critics and doubt as to the wisdom of Colchester following the lead of their neighbours in embracing professionalism.'

U's indeed had arrived. Before long there was a new covered stand at the Layer Road end and results were so consistent that by the time the return Ipswich game came around, Colchester had reached third place, two points ahead of Ipswich — one of the rare times they were in a superior position of their deadly rivals.

A scriptwriter could not have had it better and the two towns went soccer mad. On the big day, Saturday 5 February 1938, three special trains bedecked in black and amber — Colchester had to change colours — made the short journey and it was reckoned that there were 6,000 U's fans in the amazing 23,890 crowd which remains one of the biggest ever for a game outside the Football League. It was a minor sensation. Fans hung precariously from rafters and sat on top of the stands. Every vantage point was taken.

So to the game, which carried so much drama it made the first encounter look like a tea party. Colchester were coasting home leading

2-1 with just three minutes left. The black and amber army were celebrating when it happened. Before you could blink, goals by Jackie Little and Perrett gave Town a sensational victory. They scored with shots that Dunn should have saved. U's fans were dumbfounded and poor Dunn brokenhearted. He was also blamed by some for the first goal scored by Len Astill and was distraught for weeks. The former Crystal Palace 'keeper had been a bugler in the Army – the reason why the Post Horn gallop was adopted when the team ran out. Many disappointed fans never forgave poor Dunn – he certainly never forgave himself – and he was not retained, Bill Light being signed from West Brom.

The long-remembered Ipswich game might well have had a different result but for a broken leg sustained by star striker Willie Pendergast in a meaningless midweek game against Millwall Reserves the previous Monday. Willie had been a snip signing from Bristol Rovers proving to be an overnight sensation, scoring 6 goals in 4 matches. Ipswich must have been mightily relieved he was ruled out.

Manager Ted Davis had to reshuffle his attack and pondered long over an attacking replacement, finally gambling with all-purpose defender Syd Fieldus who had plied his trade with Brentford in the Football Combination. Syd was a wisecracking character and a bits and pieces player. Mainly he was a Colchester reserve. As it turned out, he proved utterly out of his depth in the steam heat of a local derby. For all that Cheyne and Pritchard nosed Colchester ahead before those final unbelievable minutes.

Fieldus became a commercial traveller and played a major role in club affairs when he was manager in the first post-war season. As for Pendergast, this striking individual who was close to being a great player eventually signed for Chester and in 1938/39, was one of the leading marksmen in the Third Division (North). The dust settled on the momentous local derby but oddly enough neither Town or U's won the Southern League. It was the highly-competent Guildford City who were champions but Ipswich won the prize that mattered, elected into the League by outvoting Gillingham at a time when they had hit stony ground and were backwater strugglers. Ipswich and all of Suffolk celebrated. It had been an amazing accomplishment and the near-24,000 crowd, plus other big gates for a series of influential friendly matches against big-named clubs were key factors.

Colchester were incensed when Town arranged one such game against Scottish aces Heart of Midlothian, the same midweek evening that Layer Road staged the Colchester Challenge Cup final between Arsenal and Wolves, which nevertheless still pulled in a mammoth 17,484 fans – this remains the third-highest gate ever.

U's ended their first-ever season by lifting the Southern League Cup beating Yeovil and then began the next campaign with Ipswich providing the tremendous counter attraction of League football. They jumped off to a fine start too, beating Southend United 4-2 at Portman Road although oddly enough it was not a full house. For all that, the 21,000 turnout was better than three in the First Division and three in the Second Division.

There was a romantic story over that game – the Southend team went to Suffolk by sea via Felixstowe. Romance also as Ipswich, after a run of poor results, finished their pioneering venture in seventh place which was a record for a club in its first season of League football. Ipswich made a habit of instant success. They also figured in some dramatic FA Cup action against Aston Villa forcing a replay after a 1-1 draw. The afternoon Portman Road replay – floodlights were unheard of – drew an incredible 28,194 crowd, a ground record for many years.

Town had to counter some questionable Villa tackling. They went down 2-1 but it might have been different but for a bad injury to Dave Bell. It meant playing with only ten men – no substitutes then either. As it was, Villa only just got home, thanks to a late Fred Haycock goal.

While Ipswich were collaring the headlines, U's reaped their own success too, winning the Southern League championship. They kept the Ipswich link going by beating Town reserves 3-2 at Portman Road on the last day of the season, former Ipswich winger Len Astill scoring the winner.

Then we had the Second World War and it was to be 1950/51 before the rivals clashed once more. There were many memorable meetings with U's usually coming off second best. An exception was 1951/52 when it was a Colchester double. At Portman Road, Vic Keeble and Fred Cutting scored in a 2-0 win and in the return which saw a 1-0 victory, the unlikely match winner was Trevor Rowlands, a former Norwich City central defender who was gambled with as a striker.

Leading up to the final was the never-to-be-forgotten goalless draw of 1957; the adversaries met twelve times in League games, Colchester won two, drew four and lost six. There was also a largely forgotten League Cup meeting in 1969/70 when Ipswich at home were 4-0 winners. It was another of those games somehow lost in the dusty pages of time.

The clubs parted ways when Ipswich dramatically won promotion by goal average in 1956/57, snatching the prize after luckless U's had led the way for the major part of the season. It was a cliffhanger of a business and if Colchester had gained the elevation, events might well have panned out differently. Colchester support was at its highest ever, and there were grandiose plans for expanding the ground to take 25,000. But it was not to be, and, in a competitive sense, the two clubs have been worlds apart ever since. A touch of envy remains. One had it with Chelmsford who were intensely jealous of United's League status. So too with Colchester and Ipswich. While United, apart from the occasional one-off highlight, slogged it out in the lower regions, Town were invariably in the ascendancy and lording it up.

They always had good managers – two subsequent knights in Sir Alf and Sir Bobby – top-line players, solid support and a pitch that looked like a billiard table. They amazingly won the two big domestic prizes, the First Division title and the FA Cup and followed by lifting the UEFA Cup. Is it any wonder that the Layer Road tannoy announcers relating half-time scores cannot hide fiendish pleasure if Town happen to be losing!

The roots of envy go back to those halcyon days of the 1930s when it all began. Young supporters of today would be amazed at the tense rivalry. However there is a strong link with player and manager moves, most of them in the Layer Road direction. Look who have occupied the U's hot seat – Cyril Lea, Mick Mills, Ian Atkins, George Burley and Steve Whitton. Burley, that dependable full-back of glory days was the most controversial. Still cutting his teeth and highly ambitious, he was unveiled by chairman Gordon Parker, who delighted in introducing new faces with a showbiz touch, Burley dramatically appearing from behind a curtain before the invited media.

Burley, who had been managing and coaching in Scotland, started indifferently but was soon riding high with U's in fifth spot after a great run. Then, at Christmas, came the bombshell of all times. What a way to ruin the festivities; Burley, who had a two-year contract, walked out to take over Ipswich from the departed John Lyall. United fans knew nothing of the shock news until turning up for the Boxing Day match against Northampton. They were nonplussed and angry.

Burley's exit created great animosity for weeks and soured relationships between the two clubs. It led to lengthy legal wrangling before eventually Colchester did receive some compensation. Player moves between Layer Road and Portman Road have been numerous – from Ray Crawford and Ted Phillips to the redoubtable Micky Stockwell. Roger Osborne, who will forever be known for his 1978 FA Cup winner, played 237 games and Bobby Blackwood, a wing half of the 1960s, made 115 appearances. Other well-known players, England defender Kevin Beattie and Trevor Whymark, pulled on the U's shirt on a handful of occasions, but you can select a pretty formidable team from ex-Townies.

When and if Colchester United and Ipswich Town meet head to head again is a debatable point. But they are now only a division apart so who knows? Meanwhile one can but savour those gripping local derbies of far-off days.

7

Post-War Blues

The Odd Season

The strangest Colchester United season of all was the immediate post-war campaign of 1945/46. Hostilities had not long ceased and the hangover of the great conflict hung on. There were still ration books and a lot of restrictions. Neither did it seem all that long since a V-1 flying bomb had crashed harmlessly in a field near the garrison which, during the war years, had housed so many well-known players. You could have compiled a vast Footballers' Who's Who from their numbers.

While the war was on, Army football had thrived, with unit teams competing for the Old Contemptibles Cup for charity. The finals were played at Layer Road where in 1943, South-Eastern Command met Eastern Command for charity and the likes of Frank Swift, Tommy Lawton, Stan Cullis and Cliff Britton were on show.

Colchester resumed in a small-scale Southern League comprising eleven teams. A League Cup tournament and friendly matches provided additional fixtures and as guest players were allowed, Colchester were immediately expected to have a big advantage. The snag was players getting leave passes, something manager Syd Fieldus, a pre-war player, would quickly encounter. Fieldus did everything, acting as secretary and sometimes playing which all in all was a thankless task, but Syd was a lovable character and did a great job. He was a commercial traveller, a wisecracking Londoner with a nice line in patter – a sort of Arthur Daley of *Minder* fame.

There was a good relationship with the local Army people but the player Fieldus would have liked for the entire campaign was Jackie Robinson, a dazzling inside forward who had won England caps. and scored twice in the memorable 6-3 win against Germany at Berlin in the 1930s. But for Colchester, he played only one major game.

Robinson, the dark-haired superstar of Sheffield Wednesday, was always challenging the likes of Jimmy Hagan, Raich Carter and Wilf Mannion, and outside of this trio, he was the best inside forward I have ever seen. Beautifully balanced, he had great ball control and pace plus a lethal finish. Jackie was very much my boyhood idol and I was thrilled to enjoy a welcoming pint with him when he first arrived in town.

It was wartime then, and Robinson starred for his unit, the 16th ITC, but he was to wear a U's shirt only twice, once against Chelmsford City and again in an Ipswich friendly. Strings were pulled in the right places and Jackie made 21 appearances for his beloved Wednesday, scoring 17 goals. Later he joined Sunderland and died at a tragically early age.

The other top name in the Colchester army ranks was Arsenal's Dave Nelson, a ball artist if ever there was one, but this skilled Scot, a rather moody dour individual, turned out for Fieldus for only three games. He later carved out a career with Fulham and Brentford. Colchester had splendid service from other less glamorous servicemen, notably central defender Jimmy Jenkins of Bristol City, West Brom defender Jimmy Southam and Ron Hornsby, a pint-sized left-winger. Jenkins missed only four games and an ever-present was Bill Bower, the sturdy former Millwall full-back. It was impossible to field a settled side and would you believe, eighty-one separate players pulled on a U's shirt that season, many just the once. Players constantly flitted from club to club like the tough Brighton striker, Albert Day, who ended up with Ipswich Town.

The season began with a 2-1 win over Chelmsford City at New Writtle Street but U's lost the return 4-3 at Layer Road a week later when Robinson did play and score. The gates were a shade over 5,000 and City were good value for their victory. They pulled a surprise cracker by playing Peter Buchanan, the flying right-winger of Chelsea fame. He and Denny Foreman scored twice after U's had led 3-1!

The entire season was a joke really. It was never anything like the real thing but something of a sham, although the crowds starved during the war years drifted back and most liked what they saw. For Fieldus it was a rollercoaster of a ride and some heavy away defeats were suffered on marathon trips of which Barry was the longest.

Journeys mostly by train were tedious and tiring and motorways did not exist. The big massacres were 8-0 maulings at Bath and Yeovil and the humiliation at Huish underlined the difficulties encountered. Six leading players were at the last minute barred from travelling and a seventh, Leeds United's Irish international Harry Browne, couldn't get away. Army Fire Service players, inexperienced and out of their depth, made up the scratch side. They held out for twenty-five minutes but then the floodgates opened and injuries saw U's end up with ten men.

It was all so frustrating, more so because that same day, Robinson and Hornsby played and scored for Ipswich against Northampton Town. The Colchester team arrived back home at 4 a.m. weary and despondent and Fieldus, who was ever an optimist, vowed he would have Robinson and other big names for the next home match against Bedford, but nothing of the sort happened.

We moan about the rail network today. Then it was an equally harrowing long-winded tedious affair and what with dawn starts, away match days were a protracted business. Fieldus was a 100 per cent Colchester – a devout enthusiast. He tried to recruit pre-war players but with not much success. Ivan Thacker, Bill Light and Cecil Allan had a handful of games but Roy Morris and George Wallis, whom he hoped to include in an FA Cup tie away to Wisbech, failed to make an appearance. Wisbech rapidly ended any cup hopes, winning 5-0 and I remember poor Syd being too stressed out to watch the rout. He left the action and wandered the streets around Fenland Park desolately.

When U's lost a 8-0 at Bath, England 'keeper Vic Woodley played. They also had Blackpool star-to-be Stan Mortensen, but mercifully he was not in the action that day. Colchester lost more games than they won but there were some encouraging displays, especially when Brentford striker Len Townsend bagged a hat-trick in a 3-1 win over Guildford City. Arsenal's well-known Welsh international Leslie Jones made a one-off appearance. Gates picked up too – 6,400 and 7,016 for local derbies against Chelmsford City while there was 5,317 for a friendly against Norwich. The real crowd-puller, however, was the star-studded showpiece representative game between Colchester Garrison and a Combined Services team boasting top-liners like Frank Swift, Tommy Lawton and Frank Soo. There was a gate close to 10,000 and playing for the Garrison was United's twenty-two-year-old forward George Barnard, subsequently sold to Arsenal for a four-figure fee. He was said to be set for big things but failed to make the grade.

Looking back it was fantasy football but it pleased a lot of people, including myself, then embarking on a sports writing career with the old weekly *Colchester Gazette*. It holds many a nostalgic memory. Chelmsford City, who had a good blend of youngsters and star guests, finished as runaway Southern League winners but bigger events were about to loom up on the Colchester United horizon. Ted Fenton, who played in that representative match, was appointed player-manager and history was about to be made.

Skipper Supreme

Reg Stewart, now a well-preserved seventy-eight-year-old, was a U's centre half between 1949 and 1957 and captain in the early Football League days. A born leader, Peter Wright, for one, reckons he was the skipper supreme.

Reg, a Yorkshireman through and through, was tall and commanding. A rare humorist and a fun-filled extrovert, there was the look of Hollywood's Jimmy Stewart about him and Reg typified the team spirit that abounded. He is best remembered for his ukelele playing on away journeys leading hearty singsongs to wile away the long hours.

This was of course a vastly different soccer world than today's highly sophisticated game. As Reg remembers, most players rode bikes or walked to games. A few of the better-paid had second-hand cars, but the main incentive was a house which was what was promised him when he moved south from Sheffield Wednesday.

Reg, born only a stone's throw from Hillsborough, had been with Wednesday for five years playing mostly for the Central League side. He had 5 first-team games and the one that lives with him most was against Newcastle United at St James' Park. The forward line included Jackie Milburn, Len Shackleton, Charlie Wayman and Tommy Pearson. Wayman gave Reg a torrid time and scored four.

Reg's father was a footballer but it was Ernie Blenkisopp, former England and Liverpool full-back, who was his mentor. He was his uncle and greatly influenced his career. Reg also recalls going to his first ever Wednesday match when the admission was two old pence and there were 40,000 spectators but only four policeman stationed at each corner of the ground.

His move to Essex came about when Bob Curry's father-in-law spotted he was on the transfer list. He phoned Bob who told Jimmy Allen and the deal was done. Stewart was listed at £3,000 but U's, being a non-League club, didn't have to pay. For Reg, it was a different world coming from, as he says, a noisy grimy industrial city to peaceful rural Essex and a town where you see trees from the window and the coast was not far away!

Reg remembers 'Colchester was a football-mad town then and while you could walk down a Sheffield street unnoticed, down Colchester High Street, everyone spoke to you.'

When he signed, his wages were £10 winter and £8 summer but Jimmy Allen set up a deal whereby he did paintwork on the ground and helped prepare a new running track. That brought it up to £10.

In 1949, one of the highlights were the local derbies with Chelmsford City and there was a big Colchester outcry when their big rivals signed well-known personalities: Joe Crozier, the Brentford 'keeper; Frank Soo, the ex-Stoke City and England international, and Cecil McCormack from Middlesbrough.

All were on big money but U's more often than not came out on top in these high-profile clashes. And they bagged a big name when Stan Foxall signed on. Reg recalls this extrovert character with nostalgia. He says, 'Rationing was still on and man about town Stan used to bring in packets of tea for the lads. He had a beaked nose and I remember a match at Dartford when he went down and someone said, "he went so far on that nose he's left a furrow!".'

That season, U's finished with 74 points but amazingly still missed out on the title which went to Merthyr. Reg remains convinced that it was the club's central geographical position that brought about to their League election and that it was team spirit and fitness that led to their opening seven-match unbeaten run. Reg likes nothing better than to spin a good soccer yarn.

On Jimmy Allen, 'He was a true gentleman, possibly not quite hard enough, but he had a dry sense of humour. During the 7-1 defeat at Plymouth, I gave away a penalty and Jim said at half-time, "We are playing eleven men and the referee and linesman and you go and play for them. Why don't you go and knock on their door and ask for one of their shirts?".'

On Benny Fenton, 'He did things his way and had his own ideas. One was man-marking and he used to tell me to follow the centre forward everywhere. If he went to the wing I had to go with him and it didn't make any difference when I argued about the middle being open. But he did bring some class to the team.'

On how the game has changed, 'The difference is with the equipment and the grounds. With the footwear as it is now I would love to be playing today. I can remember Layer Road sometimes looking like a ploughed field.'

On money in the game, 'I can remember when we were going through a bad spell and director Len Gunary said, "We badly need a result. Here is £29 between thirteen of you, the twelfth man and the trainer." We played out of our skins and won, revelling in picking up £2 extra.'

Best players? 'Bobby Hill and Sammy McLeod could do great things with a football. George Fisher was the most immaculate of full-backs, a role model and what of Vic Keeble – he had the heart of a lion and before he went to Newcastle they said here is a player who could take penalties with his head! When he went to West Ham he chased goalkeepers all over the place. Today goalkeepers have it so different. When they get the ball everyone goes away and they just roll it out.'

I like too the story of travelling to Walsall. The team had to race back to Birmingham to get the train and it was a case of a quick bath and rush for taxis. They just about made it and when Reg enquired about refreshments, Jimmy Allen told him to get some pork pies and packets of crisps – and that had to do for the rest of the day! Reg's job as captain meant he was also the go-between for management and players and he instilled a great team spirit.

They were rough, tough, but entertaining days. It was in a match at Millwall when one of their players, who was in the Vinnie Jones mould, threatened to break his leg. This was the one game when Reg was sent off and as he said, 'Even having your name taken was a slur and I got a heavy fine.'

Players in that age were just as open to temptation and Stewart and company will admit they were sometimes Jack the lads. A few pints on a Saturday night at the Castle, the then landlord club director Mark Gozzett, were commonplace occurrences – but players today would be under closer scrutiny.

At the end of the season during which he sustained a toe injury, Stewart and Les Barrell were the players not retained. A thoroughly disappointed Reg fixed himself up with Southern League Hastings which was a good deal indeed. They paid good travelling expenses and stayed at the best hotels. When he eventually called it a day he was far from sure about his future, but by accident he became involved with Paxmans Social Club and was appointed manager, breathing typical Northern spirit and life into the set up. Paxmans had a thriving work force at the time and his football prowess was still well-remembered.

Stewart ran the club for thirty-two years and is now retired. He often pondered over writing a book – it would have been titled *From Club to Club*, and he wished he had extended his after-dinner speech routines. He and his wife Maureen run an association where they love organising trips and outings.

In all, Stewart played 268 games scoring 2 goals. His first game was against Weymouth in a Southern League game at Layer Road on 20 August 1949 and his last versus Watford on 29 April 1957, this a 2-0 victory.

Stewart was one of many U's legends. My abiding memory of him is leading those rousing singsongs win or lose on a coach speeding home in the darkness and Len Jones rendering his particular favourite, which was 'Moonlight And Roses'.

Magpies Downed

Newcastle United at Layer Road? It happened in 1960 and again in 1982 but it was the first occasion that was really epoch making. Today it would be Alan Shearer and Kieron Dyer. Then it was Len White, superstar striker and Ivor Allchurch, the Welsh wizard of dribble.

Newcastle had been the wonder team in the 1950s, twice FA Cup winners beating Arsenal in 1951/52 and Manchester City three years later. They came to Layer Road in the first season of the Football League

Cup and were long odds-on favourites to dispose of a Colchester side that were in a slough of despair. There had been eight games without a win and much of the gloss and excitement of earlier Benny Fenton seasons was a memory.

Newcastle, by contrast, were very much on a high and were a powerful First Division outfit. There was a sentimental link too in that Colchester striker Vic Keeble had worn the famous black and white shirt and had won a cup-winners medal in 1955.

It was a low point in Colchester football. Gates had plummeted to 4,000 and although the Newcastle tie was 15,000 all ticket, the actual crowd on the night of Monday 10 October 1960 was a disappointing 9,130. That reflected the downbeat mood, but Fenton made wholesale changes and the result was a quite amazing 4–1 win.

Trevor Harris, a local lad, was given his debut and this highly combative wing half was an immediate success. Trevor was a no-nonsense player and we didn't always see eye to eye. Often he disagreed with my reports, but all was forgotten when we met up years later at a time when I chronicled the fabulous deeds of his son Del, who was a national squash champion.

There was an equally competitive performer in the gutsy Ronnie Hunt at left half. The enigmatical Martyn King was preferred to Neil Langman and little Sammy Mcleod who had been out of favour made a comeback.

Colchester simply dazzled. Full-backs Alf McMichael, who had figured in the 1951/52 final, and Dick Keith, a star for Ireland in an international the previous week, were given the runaround by Tommy Williams and Peter Wright. Bobby Hill and little McLeod were magical and two-goal King was utterly dynamic.

You either loved or hated King. Many fans disliked the shrug of despair when things went wrong but King on his day was a top-drawer performer who would have been close to the million pound class today. He was a classic striker of the old school and had played for ace amateurs Pegasus, a team reminiscent of the famous Corinthians who were a sensation in the 1920s.

United were off to a great start and Newcastle 'keeper Brian Harvey was to have a nightmare match. In two minutes he was all at sea dealing with a McLeod lob and Williams scored. Then King showed his class with a sizzling close dribble, leaving Heslop and Keith in his wake before providing a deadly finish. King was so often a big-occasion man.

On the stroke of half-time, the crowd were in further disbelief as King headed down a Harris free-kick and Wright clinically finished with a typical picture-book goal. In the second half a shell-shocked Newcastle pulled one back through Duncan Neale and Allchurch made one wonder run practically the whole length of the field to no avail. Newcastle lacked iron man Jimmy Scoular but had no excuses. They rated John Fowler, the dour Scot, the best left-back they had seen all season.

King popped up with his second goal and Colchester had scored a memorable victory against all the odds. It was their first win after 720 minutes of misery.

Fenton and the fans must have thought they had turned the corner, but the slump returned. The next game at home to Halifax saw a 2-1 defeat and during a woeful season there was a run of twelve games without a win and a horrendous 7-2 hammering away to Tranmere. Inevitably it led to relegation and that memorable Newcastle victory must simply go down as one of those bizarre one-off results – a fleeting oasis in a barren desert, you could say.

As it turned out, Fenton's troops regained Third Division status at the first attempt, smashing goalscoring records in the process – but that's another story. What of the second U's meeting with the Magpies? That was in 1981/82 in the FA Cup third round. At St James' Park, a Steve Wignall header earned a 1-1 draw and a Layer Road replay that was a real humdinger of thrills and spills and two penalties despatched by Ian Allinson. Newcastle won 4-3, a young Chris Waddle one of their scorers.

Magic Moments

Classic Encounters

Fulham in 1963 and Aston Villa in 1979 – these were classic encounters of a special kind.

It was Benny Fenton's last season when the Cottagers came to Layer Road for a Football League Cup tie that was to shock the football world. They had Johnny Haynes, the top inside forward of the era, Alan Mullery, Bobby Robson and George Cohen, later to star in England's World Cup triumph. What would Fayed think of that little lot? The Fulham side then would be worth millions in today's preposterous market and against little old Colchester, it was expected to be a cakewalk.

Today Fulham parade foreigners like Legwinski, Inamoto, Malbranque and Sava, names you can barely pronounce. I would have Haynes and company any day and would back them to win. They were the top stars of their era.

Yet U's won 5-3 and Fulham were reduced to mere mortals. The immaculate Haynes, the first £100 a week footballer, was something special. Probably the best distributor of a ball ever, he was in his way the David Beckham of the 1960s. Haynes could effortlessly string out inch-perfect passes as though tape-measured but on that Wednesday night, 25 September 1963, he was cut down to size, never relishing the razor sharp tackling of Duncan Forbes, Chris Rutter and Ronnie Hunt.

The odd thing was that during that season U's had, despite a strong squad, suffered a series of inconsistent results, and gates were indifferent. The season's opener against Barnsley pulled in only 3,500 fans – the lowest in the Football League that day.

So it was that the gate for Fulham was a mere 7,772 people, shamefully low for such an attraction. Those who bypassed the tie missed a treat. United were inspired from the outset and their first-half exhibition was dazzling. Outstanding was Roy McCrohan who had always shone against Colchester for Norwich City. He was a smooth, cultured midfielder.

On twenty-one minutes, Billy Stark started the rout with a delightful chipped free-kick and on thirty-one minutes, Mike Grice scorched one home after Martyn King had headed down a McCrohan free-kick. Mullery laid on a reply from Gordon Key, but a minute later Grice was flattened in the box and Bobby Hunt despatched the penalty.

On forty-eight minutes Stark, the Scottish-born striker, a bargain signing from Carlisle, finished off a Wright cross to make it four. Stark was a most colourful character and dry-witted humorist who invariably labelled opponents as impostors.

Amazingly it was 5-1 when King hit a post, collected the rebound and impudently walked the ball in. Fulham then saved a little face as Dave Metchick pulled a couple back but it was a subdued coach journey home. Fulham had expected it to be a cakewalk. Oddly enough, six years later, Haynes wore a Colchester shirt when alongside clubmate Johnny Byrne. He guested for U's in a testimonial for former Fulham goalkeeper, the flashy Tony Macedo. The match was part of the deal that took Macedo from Craven Cottage and it was against a full-strength Ipswich side who won 6-2 before a very good gate of 4,515. Alas, Colchester, after beating Fulham, only occasionally repeated that form and it was an odd season of highs and lows.

Just before the Fulham night of high jinks, U's had lost 5-4 at Wrexham, crashed 4-0 to Peterborough and the deadly Derek Dougan one week and reversed it with a 4-1 Layer Road victory a week later. There were also fine wins against the big-money sides. Queens Park Rangers and Coventry City and Fenton had a very good squad – goal men Hunt, King and Stark plus ace wingers Grice and Wright.

For all that, there was always the search for new faces. Enquiries were made about Ipswich Town crack-shot Ted Phillips and there was talk of a possible exchange deal involving Bobby Hunt, but Phillips said he wanted a higher grade of football although he was to come two years later.

United reserves at this time found it hard-going in the powerful Football Combination and were slaughtered 9-4 by Spurs at White Hart Lane, Tottenham parading Welsh international Mel Hopkins and first-team striker Les Allen.

Then came Benny's departure back to an old East London haunt at Leyton Orient and U's gave him a fine farewell, winning a first-round FA Cup tie at Brighton with a brilliantly typical goal – that kind you rarely see today. Wright shimmied and weaved his way to the byline, cut the ball back and Hunt had merely to slide it home. QPR applied the knockout in the second round and with the arrival of Franklin, a disappointing seventeenth placing was achieved and it was a campaign remembered primarily for Fulham.

Sixteen years later were more cup thrills of a very different kind. For the first time ever, United played at Villa Park and in ninety minutes won 2-0 – the only time U's have won outright on a First Division or Premiership ground, but they lost the match, a second-round League Cup tie, 9-8 on penalties!

It was the most extraordinary and totally unexpected of nights for Colchester had been beaten in the home first leg 2-0 and it was all expected to be a non-event formality. Villa Park was less than half full with a crowd of 19,473 but as Martin Smith wrote in his *Essex County Standard* report: "Patrons in the glass-fronted hospitality boxes choked on their champagne as Bobby Gough scored from a Bobby Hodge cross and they were nonplussed again when the panther-like Trevor Lee levelled on aggregate, Steve Wignall making the opening."

Colchester were a totally different side to that beaten at Layer Road when Tony Morley and Gary Shaw were the match-winners. Mike Walker brought off superb saves and U's went close to sealing the issue before extra time.

The Villa faithful just couldn't believe it and the penalty shoot-out that followed was full of high-noon tension and jangling nerves, one of the most protracted ever. There were saves by both keepers and several re-takes before, an hour after the end of normal time, it was finally decided when Walker blazed his kick high over. Utterly heartbreaking for the underdogs who had gone so close to a major upset and manager Bobby

Roberts revealed afterwards that during his playing career he had never been associated with a losing side at Villa Park.

There have arguably been better Villa sides but winger Morley, who later picked up six England caps, was rated at £200,000 and Gary Shaw and John Deehan were high-profile performers.

It was a handy Colchester side too. Popular Steve Leslie and Steve Foley were still going strong and the defence was solid with the likes of Wignall, Mick Packer and Steve Dowman, whose outrageous hairstyle rivalled the Afro mode of Trevor Lee.

Promotion that season in fact looked a fair bet but was missed due to a poor run-in. They saw a fifth spot realised, six points behind third-placed Sheffield Wednesday, but above all else it was a campaign when that Villa Park duel to the death was the highlight.

Money, Money Money

In September 2000, Colchester United were really in the money – jackpot winners in a big way. Lomana Lua Lua was transferred to Premiership giants Newcastle United for £2.25 million. It was for the U's a historic day and it was a far cry from 1953 when Vic Keeble signed for the same Newcastle for £15,000 – a fortune in those days.

Lua Lua was U's first million-pound-plus player but, in point of fact, there were others on the Premiership circuit in the class. There were Mark Kinsella and Martin Grainger, who was surely worth £1 million in his early, stunning Birmingham City days. Both players were, in my view, grossly undersold. Kinsella went to Charlton Athletic in 1996 for just over £125,000 with several strings attached. The much-capped Irishman has probably expanded that figure to around £300,000 – but in any event, Charlton got a bargain. Kinsella performed on the World Cup stage with distinction and is now with West Brom after a spell at Aston Villa – and I still think was underpriced!

Birmingham came out of it well too with Grainger whom Colchester sold to Brentford for £30,000. Grainger developed into one of the best defenders in the Nationwide League.

Martin will always be remembered for an Autoglass cup tie at Layer Road when he potted the first goal from the penalty spot. He was not the regular spot-kick man and the bookmaker on the ground who had offered a generous price suffered a mauling!

There was never any doubt that Kinsella would make the big time. The stylish midfielder is an unassuming delightful character and a fine example to any up-and-coming youngster, and credit must go to the late Jock Wallace who snapped him up from the Dublin club Home Farm.

Wallace also earned the club quick cash in one extraordinary deal. He signed left-winger Paul McGee from Bohemians but the player was at Layer Road for only three weeks and four games before Wimbledon bought him for £75,000. Later bonus payments brought the sum to around £125,000 and this was a Colchester record for some years, outstripping the £90,000 Gillingham paid for Trevor Lee in 1981.

The other big transfer deal was in 1994 when Steve McGavin went to Birmingham for £150,000. He had originally cost £10,000 and the then Birmingham boss Barry Fry had long been keen on the talented striker. Steve, one of the nicest players you could wish to meet was, to me, something of an enigma and fell just short of being a top-stage performer. He never made it at St Andrews, went to Wycombe Wanderers and then non-League with Dagenham & Redbridge.

Steve's best football was unquestionably at Colchester and he was a big factor in the Conference-Trophy double season. Like Kinsella, he loves to come back visiting to Layer Road.

Back to today and the incredible Lua Lua whom Bobby Robson has predicted will be another George Best. The credit for launching his career and netting the club a small fortune must go to Geoff Harrop who spotted him playing for Leyton College.

Lua Lua has profited immensely from being carefully groomed and handled. He was gradually introduced by Steve Whitton and used first as substitute before becoming a regular starter. Robson at St James' Park has adopted a similar policy but Lua Lua began to have some full games marking them with his first Premiership goals and that trademark celebration double somersault.

His Layer Road stay was short – 63 appearances and 18 goals – but he is arguably the most popular and most talked-about Colchester player ever. Local crowds had never seen anything quite like it before – bewildering breathtaking skills from U's first player from the Third World. The question remains – was he undersold? Time alone will tell.

What of the future? Well obviously Colchester could use another Lua Lua lottery-type windfall. Steve Whitton always pinned his hope on that and unearthing young talent in a tough Division Two where he had to compete with the likes of Cardiff City who have been backed to the hilt by mega-money magnates. Ironically, the only time Colchester did have a tycoon-styled benefactor, they went down a stony road that led to the non-League wilderness.

But at the end of the day, cash is the keyword. The collapse of ITV Digital was a major blow but the Sky TV deal has eased the situation. Now what is badly needed is the new stadium to generate fresh income. Then and only then can Colchester begin to think of advancement with any real optimism.

I would say almost exclusively that U's are the most prudently operated League club in the country, and that's to the credit of chairman Peter Heard who in the TV digital dispute emerged as a key figure. But U's do deserve more tangible support. This was always a sore point with Whitton who questioned as to whether Colchester was really football-minded. When there was a game at Wembley, 20,000 supporters arrived from nowhere. Yet the hardcore bread-and-butter League support has dwindled to 3,500.

Time was when it was 5,000 to 6,000 and 5,000 was a gate to worry about, but one must remember of course that then it was a vastly different game. There were never as many other counter-attractions and in an unsophisticated world people invariably stuck by their team. Today, by contrast, we have countless distractions and teenagers have money enough to follow their big club favourites the length and breadth of the country. U's put against Manchester United and Arsenal are just small beer.

Of course U's do have some splendid supporters and you have to admire the loyal band that regularly hit the road for away games. There is also a fringe contingent ready and waiting for a big success run, and the 6,000 crowd for Richard Wilkins' testimonial against Spurs proved that the big occasion game will pull them in.

There is no doubt in my mind that the biggest benefactor to Colchester United should be the local council. But for decades now they have dithered and dallied over that much-needed new ground. In my view they have been little short of disgraceful as so many other clubs have benefited and continue to benefit from modern all-purpose stadia befitting the twenty-first century. What never seems to dawn on the local authorities is the fact that Colchester United are members of an exclusive club. And the prestige importance when their name comes out with the soccer results every Saturday cannot be overestimated.

Let's hope that new stadium is not far away this time. Meantime, all of us will keep hoping for another mammoth Lua Lua lotto win!

Other Games Remembered

The Norwich City derbies, while not quite so epic as Ipswich Town confrontations, were big occasions and Colchester had a fair record at Carrow Road. They gained a 1-1 draw there in their first season before a mammoth 25,669 spectators and scored memorable victories in 1954/55 and 1956/57. And the next season, a classic, another 1-1 draw, sticks in my mind. The 1950s was a lovely soccer decade and a rail excursion up to Norfolk was a special event and thrill.

In the old days for Ipswich, derbies trains were decked out in the colours and seen off by the stationmaster. That tradition had gone but there was still a buzz and the tug of anticipatory excitement as the fans sped through the East Anglian countryside. This match in question, Saturday 18 January 1958, was a superb piece of entertainment from every angle. As I wrote at the time, 'Jet pace from two of the fittest outfits in the Third Division almost broke the sound barrier.' Carrow Road, with 17,523 excited fans, was quite a sight. It's a modern-styled all-seat stadium today but, as with most new grounds, I find there is not the old atmosphere. There was plenty that January afternoon as two fine teams battled it out. Old man Benny Fenton was still going strong and, from the outset, riled the locals.

There was a incident right in front of the grandstand involving City's Ralph Hunt, who had his name taken. It was like waving a red flag at a bull and the crowd bawled out Benny from thereon, but he had the last laugh as was so often the case. Hunt opened the scoring in the 11th minute, but Ken Plant's header left Ken Nethercott clawing air for a 30th minute equaliser.

From thereon, U's had the edge and subdued a very good City side that boasted the likes of ball-playing wizards Johnny Gavin and Bobby Brennan. Fenton was irrepressible over the last fifteen minutes. Head down, he brushed by defenders in a twenty-yard dash to the byline. The end result was three successive corners which all but brought the Colchester winner.

The Layer Road Norwich derby clash that was one for the scrapbook was the 1960 3-0 win that really left City smarting. It was Martyn King's game with a storybook hat-trick, the first timed at twenty-four seconds. That goal, graphically recorded by photographer Des Blake, provided a sequel picture of five U's players hugging and embracing which prompted the question as to over-the-top hysterics.

How the game has changed. Those celebrations were tame compared with the ugly shirt-removing antics of today which would have caused an outrage. That twenty-four-second opener, which is a record, is worthy of ball-by-ball description. Neil Langman kicked off, passing to Bobby Hill who transferred to winger Tommy Williams. He was checked by Ron Ashman conceding a throw-in. Derek Parker took this and Williams crossed for King to flick over Sandy Kennon's shoulder into the net. Kennon and wing half Roy McCrohan later moved to Layer Road and gave excellent service.

Quick on the draw, King's other goals were fine shots on the run and it was his third hat-trick of a season where he could do little wrong. Few of the others could either. Bobby Hill was a brilliant schemer and little Williams' trickery frequently left poor Ashman floundering on his backside. Percy Ames, who only played after a late fitness test, made some fine saves against this very good City side which was in the running for promotion, something they ultimately achieved, finishing second to Southampton. That made Colchester's win even more praiseworthy. They themselves ended ninth but on that Layer Road afternoon, they appeared a promotion bet and the crowd was 13,053. The games that season were the last competitive clashes with the Canaries – City won 3-2 at Carrow Road. Will they ever return? And will Colchester ever exceed their record tall scoring wins – 9-1 against Bradford City and 8-2 v. Stockport County? Both were extraordinary, the Stockport massacre on Saturday 9 October 1958 predominately because it featured a Sammy McLeod hat-trick – and a goal from the pint-sized Scot was something of a rarity too. The twinkle-toed schemer was invariably a goal-maker but that afternoon the man who was the provider was sleek part-timer Russell Blake – five of the eight came from his crosses. Lofty John Evans emulated McLeod's hat-trick and 6ft-plus Neil Langman hit a brace. U's put on a ruthless all-attacking show and had the killer touch. I thought they were about to declare at 4-1 but County's Welsh international winger Roy Clarke jolted them out of a casual spell with a shot that rebounded in off a post.

The previous best wins had been sixes at the expense of Walsall and Shrewsbury, but it was Bradford City who were hit for nine. The odd thing here was that City had won 4-1 at Valley Parade on Boxing Day. The return at a muddy Layer Road three days later on Saturday 30 December 1961 saw Bobby Hunt and Martyn King hit four apiece. The other scorer was little Bobby Hill who waved the magician's wand with a superlative display of inside-forward play. He was the midfield foreman in undisputed charge, twisting the hapless City defence inside out with dazzling ball control and then splitting it wide open with tape-measured passes to both wings and down the middle. With wingers Mike Foster and Peter Wright also in sparkling form, Hunt and King just couldn't fail yet after Hill's opening goal — it was 1-1 when Barrie Tait scored and there was never a hint of the rout to follow.

Six of the goals came in the last twenty-five minutes and it was an eye-catching treat for the 4,415 crowd. Foster was an underrated winger who came from Leicester and this was his one season before he moved on to Norwich. He played 40 games, scored 9 goals and his ninety minutes against Bradford were arguably his best. One lost count of the time he tight-roped along the byline to lay on perfect passes. But before and after the high jinks of that murky December afternoon, it was a bumper scoring campaign in which 110 League and Cup goals were chalked up.

Peterborough could definitely be termed bogeymen. There were invariably more defeats than wins when Posh were met. One of the rare victories at London Road was in 1970/71 when Roy Massey sealed a 2-1 success with a remarkable solo goal. Peterborough were, of course, a famed giant-killing cup outfit when in the Midland League and were admitted to the Football League on the back of some stirring cup performances. They just got the better of U's in a first round saga in 1961/62. It started at London Road with a 3-3 draw, U's coming back from the dead with goals from Brian Abrey, Bobby Hunt and Peter Wright. A crowd of 16,469 saw this thriller and there was a 10,653 Layer Road gate for the replay.

Bobby Hunt was hitting the heights at this stage. He laid on a goal for Martyn King and it appeared he had shot Colchester through with a typically brash effort, but livewire Dennis Emery squeezed out a desperately late equaliser and it stayed at 2-2 after extra time. The lanky Emery had been one of Posh's famed cup fighters for a number of years.

The second replay was at Carrow Road and was sheer anti-climax. U's were handicapped when Martyn King was ruled out by injury and the gamble of playing Sammy McCleod at number nine flopped. Posh also missed Emery, who was critically ill in hospital after a car crash, but George Hudson, a £4,000 bargain buy from Accrington, made up for Emery's loss with a first-half hat-trick. Terry Bly, the old Norwich favourite, was still going strong and played a major role in Peterborough's 3-0 win. They went on to the fourth round, beating Newcastle at St James' Park en route.

Another bleak season was 1966/67 when Peterborough won both League games – 4-1 at Layer Road – and further administered a 3-0 FA Cup defeat also at a wintry Layer Road. The rout was started via a horrendous own goal from Mick Loughton, but this sturdy central defender certainly had more good games than bad ones. He was a homely honest character who had a smallholding at Layer and there was the sniff of the country about him. In all, Mick played 133 Colchester games and later moved to Chelmsford City where he had two spells as manager.

An unusual game in the scrapbook of memories cropped up in Colchester's first Conference season. In the FA Trophy they drew Wivenhoe Town, the village club who overnight had become a sensational success. They had a new well-equipped ground at Broad Lane and with financial backing, possessed high ambitions. At the time they were riding high in the Vauxhall Opel League and were managed by ex-U's record-breaker Micky Cook.

The tie was of great novelty interest and there was a near-5,000 Layer Road crowd, some expecting an upset result. A defeat for U's would indeed have been a calamity but they made no mistakes. Roy McDonough opened the scoring in the twenty-fifth minute and with Ian Atkins and that will-of-the-wisp inside forward Eamonn Collins pulling the strings, it ended 3-0 with Gary Bennett bagging a brace.

Wivenhoe, whose aspirations waned in subsequent years, battled well, and Martin Gittins twice went close after a brilliant work by evergreen winger Keith Bain. Games in more recent years that stick in the mind were the 6-3 romp at Chesterfield and a never to be forgotten nine-goal thriller against Bristol Rovers in January 2000. This Layer Road rollercoaster had to be seen to be believed; Rovers, who had won eight of their previous nine games were sauntering to victory at 3-1, and second spot in Division Two beckoned. A missed penalty – Jamie Cureton's effort cannoned off the bar – was the turning point. Cureton had earlier converted from the spot and crack-shot Jason Roberts had twice been on target, but United, who had Ipswich Town's Titus Bramble on loan, struck back. Karl Duguid scored twice in two minutes, the second a stupendous volley. Steve McGavin also scored twice but it was 4-4 when Nathan Ellington was on target. Then with the 4,400 crowd breathless, Lomana Lua Lua, on as substitute, made it a 5-4 victory with a deflected shot in the dying seconds. It's not often they come as dramatic as this.

Nostalgia Unlimited

Random Thoughts

One of the least-remembered managers was Jack Butler who was in charge between the times when Jimmy Allen and Benny Fenton managed United. Butler stayed for two years – lean seasons it must be said, for they led to applications for re-election. Butler was a distinguished man who had been an outstanding Arsenal player in the 1920s and was a member of the Wembley side sensationally beaten by Cardiff City in the 1926/27 final. In the management field he had had spells with Torquay and Crystal Palace and had made a name for himself abroad by coaching the Belgian national side. He arrived at Layer Road from being in charge of Royal Daring FC.

My first impressions were good. I recall going to Layer Road for an initial interview on the most bitter of winter days and Butler, always the kindest of men, put a protective arm around my shoulders and insisted we went to his house where, before a blazing fire, he provided hot cups of tea.

Butler was not everyone's idea of a good manager, and Peter Wright thought him an oddity to say the least. He recalls the first team meeting which Butler began by throwing a packet of cigarettes on the table – they were readily snapped up. 'Then he had me out on the pitch for three hours just crossing the ball time after time', Peter also remembers. And there was the funny story of right-winger Cliff Birch. In a practice match, Butler told him, 'Just keep going and imagine there is no full-back there'. After a while, Birch ruefully said, 'That's ok boss but if there's no full-back there, who keeps kicking me?'

Butler's ideas of training and tactics bewildered a lot of the players. Results were generally poor and his health deteriorated, culminating in a nervous breakdown and his release on amicable terms. For all the lack of success, Butler had some very good players at his disposal. Bert Barlow was still a great inside forward remembered, of course, for his FA Cup performance and goal for Portsmouth against Wolves in 1939. He might have gone on to great things but for the intervention of war. For the U's, he gave many a sparkling display, often making a nonsense of his years.

In the 1960s, Bert's son Peter made his soccer bow at the age of sixteen, just twelve months after leaving school. He played on the right wing against Bournemouth but he never really made it at Layer Road and had only 23 games, ultimately going to Workington. Bert's career ended with Crittall Athletic although he still played for ex-Colchester United elevens when he was in his fifties.

Butler also signed Kenny Plant and Bob Dale from Bury and they proved to be good buys. Plant, twenty-seven years old when he arrived, was a dependable phlegmatic type, a most consistent scorer. He had scored 84 goals before he went back to his Midland roots with Nuneaton. The other season he was back at Layer Road as a guest and frankly didn't look a lot older! I am pretty sure Plant and Dale and goalkeeper Jimmy Kirk have been the only players to have been signed from Gigg Lane.

Dale came as a forward and soon made a mark, but Fenton converted him into a midfielder and he was one of the best in the lower divisions until, out of the blue, he was struck down with tuberculosis. It was the height of United's promotion challenge of 1956/57 in which Bob had played a major role. TB at that time was a dire illness and I visited Bob in a Salford hospital to cheer him up and tell him of the latest Layer Road events. He also suffered a horrific car crash which left him badly scarred with facial injuries. Happily, he fully recovered and lives locally.

Lowestoft-born Mike Grice was another originally under Butler's wing but won fame and fortune with West Ham. They paid £10,000 for him, a deal involving the Fentons. Ted was then Upton Park boss and he had just sold England B winger, Harry Hooper, to Wolves for £25,000.

Grice, who later came back to Colchester for a second spell, was a skilful winger, most magical on his day. It's funny how one remembers players for certain games. I see him as a shining light in a 2-1 win against Queens Park Rangers at the old White City which produced three of the most eye-catching goals you could ever wish for – Peter Wright and Andy Malcolm got the others.

The vast White City arena was more than half empty with the gate a mere 7,688, but U's surprised a strong Rangers side that included stars Mark Lazarus and Stuart Leary. Grice scored a scorcher from the edge of the box and then laid on the winner for Wright. Grice shot to prominence on a tour to Holland and Jimmy Allen immediately signed him. He had the occasional beer but was not one for nightlife. Wright, who played countless games with Grice on the right wing said, 'He liked to relax and rest a lot to conserve his energy. On his day he was brilliant.'

Colchester never seemed to be short of good wingers – Tommy Williams, Russell Blake, Mick Mahon, Jim Oliver, Arthur Kaye, Peter Wright, Ian Allinson, Perry Groves, Colin Garwood – the list seems endless. Kaye is not well-remembered but, when he was with Middlesbrough, he was close to an England cap. Garwood was a showman and scored some explosive goals, and Groves, who is still a frequent Layer Road spectator, was sheer speed. One remembers him most for any game against Southend.

Perhaps it was the sea air but Perry always turned it on at Roots Hall. He seemed to hold some sort of Indian sign over Southend teams of his day. Oliver, a Franklin signing from Norwich, was more often than not used as a sub, especially by Dick Graham. He would trot on with a glint in his eye and in an instant, would galvanise a crowd and turn a match.

There are many things I regret about the changed face of soccer. I detest the constant change of playing strips and the break from traditional colours and I am not over keen with most of the new modern stadiums, necessary that they are. Practical and stereotyped, they lack much in atmosphere. In the old days, for all their inadequacies, grounds had character.

Furthermore, there is the disappearance of wing play, which seems to be a forgotten art. There were few better Layer Road sights than a Williams or a Blake jetting their way to the byline on the always-popular right-hand side of the ground in full view of a packed grandstand.

Think of the many players who were really one offs. There are more than you imagine. In 1956, when U's met Ipswich in a Portman Road

Derby over Christmas, Benny Fenton, for some unknown reason, replaced Ken Plant with Alf Noble, a Leytonstone forward. Amateur football was very popular then and Noble was an international – but he simply didn't come off in a 3-1 defeat and never played again. Wing half David Buck, goalkeeper David Laitt and Des Kelly were among others who played only once and it's surprising that Dennis Hillman of the 1948 giant-killers made only four Football League appearances.

Injury was the key factor with some. Striker Paul Aimson came from Bournemouth for big money and with a high reputation. Five games and two goals later, he was a costly full-term casualty. Former Ipswich and England headliner Kevin Beattie returned to the limelight in 1983 but so briefly. The defender played five games before injury meant he had to quit for good. In the 1950s, Jimmy Allen signed defender Bill Rochford, a high-profile Wembley cup winner with Portsmouth in 1939 – but he made only two appearances.

But the 'now you see him, now you don't' theme is best illustrated by the manager who never was. After Jimmy Allen left in 1952, the board decided to appoint Ron Meades who had claimed to be player-manager of Wadebridge Town of the South Western League, but the credentials of Meades were challenged by *Essex County Standard* soccer writer Arthur Wood, and within days, his contract was cancelled.

It was a sensational story and Meades had even chaired a players' meeting the day after his appointment. What amazes me is the naivety of the Colchester board in the first place. There were big names on the short list including Arsenal's Les Henley and Peter Carey of Manchester United. It ended with egg on the faces of the directors concerned and was the most embarrassing event in Colchester United history.

Who was the Colchester player who changed his name by deed poll? Arthur Longbottom, who had been a prominent Queens Park Ranger, became Arthur Langley and was signed in 1964. A colleague and myself promptly dubbed him Langbottomly! He was a handy player and the game I always associate with him was a soccer journalist's nightmare. It was against Bournemouth and with ten minutes left, U's turned a 3-1 deficit into a 4-3 victory, Langley scoring two of them.

A player who should maybe have changed his name but didn't was Dennis Longhorn who had been with Sunderland and Aldershot. He was a wing half. Equally immaculate in action and off the pitch, Dennis was one of the most gentlemanly players I encountered.

Each soccer decade throws up special memories, many dimmed by time. Central defenders have been many and renowned and special favourites are Duncan Forbes and Stuart Morgan, a solid-as-rock no-nonsense performer with the happiest of dispositions even when barracked unmercifully on opposition grounds which was a frequent event. Stuart was sent off more than once but I felt he too often unfairly emerged as the guilty party. At Elm Park against Reading, his former club, he was baited repeatedly and the crowd eventually got their way, Stuart receiving his marching orders. It was a disgraceful business of fans influencing a referee.

Generally United teams have had good disciplinary records and in, the early days, a sending off was something of a sensation, especially before the war. When Billy Barraclough, the temperamental ex-Chelsea winger, and hard man George Wallis were sent off, there was a great outcry. It was regarded as a cardinal sin, but today, red cards have become commonplace.

Did you know, by the way, that Peter Wright in his twelve-year United career was booked only once — by the well-known one-armed referee Alf Bond?

Recalling strikers down the decades, Kevin McCurley, with his film-star looks was adored by the groupie girls of the day, and was one of my big favourites. One couldn't keep track of the times top-line clubs were in for him. But Kevin, who was also a superb golfer, never moved. John Froggatt, Bobby Svarc, the ever-consistent Tony Adcock and Bobby Gough were all crack-shots, and then there was barrel-chested Dave Simmons, one of the Leeds heroes. He too was the subject of a freak accident when he slipped down some stairs and crashed into a plate-glass door. His injuries were, at one stage, life threatening. My indelible memory of Simmons is when he was engulfed by fans behind the Layer Road end goal after the third strike that was the final nail in the Leeds coffin. It underlined the closeness between spectators and the play, but can you imagine the intimacy when there were ringside seats, as against Bradford in 1948. It was surprising that they were allowed and it was something of a mockery when a winger took a corner.

There have of course been moments of tragedy and sadness. One remembers the former Cambridge United striker John Lyons who, often unfairly barracked, became so depressed he took his own life. And then there was John Fowler, a forward who developed into an outstanding full-back, one of the fastest in the lower divisions. John, a great crowd favourite who played 442 games, collapsed and died in the arms of Peter Wright having suffered a heart attack during an ex-United players' match.

There were humorous and more uplifting moments worth remembering as well. Peter Wright and the loss of his contact lenses with the subsequent lengthy search is one, and the late Brian Hall's sham performance, following what looked like a serious injury and which earned him the nickname of Oscar for overacting, is another. There was the dog invasion that led to Brentford goalkeeper Chic Brodie being badly injured. Not that poor Brodie thought it amusing. Players' antics always entertain, as when Brian Westlake, in his enthusiasm over scoring, uprooted a corner flag and brandished it in the air. More latterly we had the exhilarating double somersaults from little Scott McGleish when he chalked up another goal. Long may it be so.

The Press Connection

Colchester United have always had a good press but it was its very best in the 1940s and 1950s when there were far more national newspapers and the sports pages devoted considerable space to lower division clubs. The old *News Chronicle* and *Daily Herald* were fine examples. There were also three London evening papers, the *Star*, the *Evening Standard* and *Evening News* all carrying reports of U's games in their Saturday afternoon football specials. Only the *Standard* has survived and so many other papers have gone to the wall – the *Sunday Pictorial*, *Sunday Empire News*, *Sunday Graphic* and the *Daily Sketch* to name a few.

Enthusiasts regularly queued for the Ipswich *Green 'Un*, which is happily still going strong although many similar Saturday night Greens and Pinks have disappeared in the face of today's instant radio and television coverage, and of course we also now have the internet and soccer websites. The *Green 'Un* has long been an institution and the *East Anglian Daily Times'* sports coverage equally impressive from its so-comprehensive reporting of the 1930s to its modern format today.

Many top-line writers have graced the Layer Road press box. Ian Woolridge, today's number one sport columnist of the *Daily Mail*, covered several games for the *News Chronicle*. So too did leading Fleet Street writers of their day Desmond Hackett and Frank Butler.

I recall the splendid *News Chronicle* pre-match coverage of the momentous Colchester *v.* Ipswich clash of 1957. There was a whole page presentation with autographed player pictures of both clubs.

Former Arsenal soccer stars Bernard Joy and Joe Hulme covered big games. Joy, writing first for the *Star* and then the *Evening Standard*, took part also in practice games before big cup ties. Hulme for a big FA Cup tie against WBA composed his report from the terraces as he was squeezed out of an over-crowded press box!

Today the nationals tend to ignore the lower divisions which is a shame. The saturation coverage is for the Premiership and I have to say I find it all a little over the top. After the World Cup, it was so tedious to read daily back-page headlines day after day revolving around Terry Venables, Roy Keane or Rio Ferdinand.

Local soccer writers have been many and make up a distinguished list. Pre-war, there were Tommy Crump and Fred Draycott, and a 1940s star was Alan Everett, then of the *Essex County Telegraph* who later teamed up with the *East Anglian Daily Times*. Alan had great flair and brilliantly reported the 1948 cup run. He was hard-hitting and fearless and Ted Fenton once threatened to ban him from matches – I experienced a similar situation with Benny Fenton.

Alan was an accomplished cricketer with Colchester and Essex and often I remember that he challenged U's players to sprint tests and, on occasions, beat them! He sometimes upset the players too by his criticism and there was an occasion when they intended to throw him in the bath! There was also dependable Arthur Wood of the *Colchester Gazette* and *Essex County Standard*, a quiet-spoken and gentlemanly Scot and Hal Mason. He was a bluff Yorkshireman who had an encyclopaedic football knowledge and owned a vast soccer memorabilia collection. Hal was a press box legend and as much a club PRO as a reporter, sharing programme editorship with me down the years. Hal did many a radio broadcast and one faux pas has gone down in history. Over came his words at half-time, 'Here at Layer Road it's a thriller. The score is 1-1 – just one lump of sugar in my tea please.' We have all been guilty of slip-ups, especially busy freelancers in a pressure world of deadlines. Many an intro has been torn up thanks to a late goal or two. A famous 5-4 win over Bristol

Rovers in a recent season was one such game and the pressures intensified as the Bristol win featured in the Sunday papers' first editions.

The work of a freelancer is hectic. He covers a game for several papers, different angles are required and manager and player quotes all quickly needed. Soccer reporting now is different in that post-match observations and interviews plus quotes are essential. In the old days, it was more a case of a lengthy almost kick-by-kick report.

Essex County Standard and *Colchester Evening Gazette* sports writers make an imposing list: Peter Hills, Robin Frost, Peter Jones, Neil Thomas, Dick Barton, Howard Walker, Bob Wailing, Derek Davis, Matt Plummer, Simon McEnnis and, of course, Frances Ponder. Enthusiastic Frances, a late entry to journalism, is a Des Lynam lookalike and a bubbling personality. He does a great job, also acting well as summariser to Des Kelly whose BBC Essex commentaries provide first-rate coverage both home and away. An occasional but always welcome press box visitor is freelancer Paul Newton, a great raconteur and best known for his superb cricket commentaries for BBC Essex, but he has always been a big U's man.

East Anglian Daily Times colleagues down the years include Bruce Jackson, who went on to make a name for himself a as racing journalist, and Robert Hadgraft, who contributes much to today's excellent match day programme. Neil Manning and the current man, amiable Carl Marston were efficient and completely unflappable. A devoted marathon runner, Carl was always the most companionable of colleagues on away trips. While he was not a journalist, Frank Rowlands must still have a mention. He contributed to the programme for many years under the nom de plume of Terracite and also produced some excellent club handbooks in the 1950s. Then he wrote *Giant-Killers*, a book on the 1947/48 cup run and other big matches. It was a good read.

Photographers such as Maurice Nichols of the *County Telegraph*; Des Blake, Dave Higgleton and Tony Tasker of the *Colchester Express* and Laurie Honeyball and Ken Goodwin of the *Standard* were first class and Des had that special knack of capturing the goals and big incidents. Some of his pictures featured in this book were brilliant, especially a match against Norwich City.

Ray Horsnail, who was with the *Essex Chronicle*, covered the famous cup tie against Everton and there are some striking examples of his work on other pages. Then there was cartoonist Ray McCluskey who went under the nom de plume Mac. His caricatures in the *Colchester Express* were first rate and could have graced a national paper. He also drew and designed the covers of United handbooks.

There has always been splendid coverage from Anglia TV. All their top men have been at Layer Road from time to time. The fine work of Essex Hospital Radio must also be mentioned – Reg Casbolt was a big champion of that worthy cause.

In all, I can say there has been impartial and fair coverage, although that cannot always be said of visiting pressman who sometimes completely take over the box as did Cardiff one season. The most biased by far seemed to me to be Wycombe and Altrincham in the Conference days.

The Layer Road press box has been like a second home to me since first reporting under the nom de plume Wanderer for the old *Colchester Gazette*. There have been great games and happy memories. Now a brand-new media centre in the new stadium is eagerly awaited.

The Very Best

Colchester United's best ever line-up? That's something for discussion over a pint or two and we would of course all come up with different teams. It's all relative but how do you compare players from so many decades. The old timers who remember the 1937 to 1939 era will swear by Alex Cheyne, but who's to say he was better than Lomana Lua Lua?

First things first, my goalkeeping choice would be the urbane and so-consistent Mike Walker. He had good penalty box command and the knack of pulling off astonishing reflex saves, and was invariably a big occasion man. In all, Mike made 522 U's appearances, while my close second-choice, Percy Ames, played 423 games. The other contenders must include Graham Smith, one of the big heroes of the Leeds triumph, flashy Tony Macedo and steady George Wright. But Walker it has to be.

Defence and I plump for a back three of George Fisher, Duncan Forbes and Brian Hall with Benny Fenton in a dual defence-midfield role. Fisher, cool and efficient, was a masterful positional full-back and a wonderful passer of the ball, but he gets the vote only narrowly over record-breaker Micky Cook who played an incredible 695 games. At central defence with the number five shirt, I must have craggy Duncan

Forbes. That means overlooking the likes of Ted Fenton, Chick Milligan and Reg Stewart. It is a close-run thing, but Duncan's approach was so inspiring. I reckon one Fenton is enough for leadership and inspiration, and Forbes, a giant of a player, hated to lose at anything — even if it was tiddly-winks. One of his best games was to completely blot out the late great Jeff Astle in the classic West Brom FA Cup tie. It was infinitely better to have big Duncan on your side than against you. Then we have Brian Hall who came from Mansfield as a left-winger but developed into what we call a wing-back today. Brian, one of the heroes against Leeds, had phenomenal pace and was the overlap specialist. There was nothing more exhilarating than Brian jetting to the byline and whipping over a lethal cross. I always remember Ray Crawford, after scoring from such a move in the unforgettable Rochdale cup replay, racing over to kiss his left boot!

Benny Fenton, in his dual role, Mark Kinsella and Lua Lua also with a roving commission are musts. Benny, a great motivator, would be skipper. Kinsella, a highly rated midfielder, was one of the most adored U's players ever and the same can be said of the remarkable Lua Lua, of whom the best is still to come. Bobby Robson, no less, forecasts he could be a second George Best.

I have a ten-match qualification rule for my top eleven so that would mean omitting the sparkling Jackie Robinson who played just one game in the first post-war season. The Sheffield Wednesday ace was outside of Raich Carter and Wilf Mannion, the greatest inside forward I ever clapped eyes on. Also ruled out is England defender Kevin Beattie who made just four appearances in the late twilight of his career.

My team is completed by front performers Bob Curry, Vic Keeble, Alex Cheyne and Peter Wright. Curry, neat and compact, was a super ballplayer who could also readily score goals. For his major role in the 1948 giant-killing run, he gets the vote. Cheyne is a pre-war choice but he was undoubtedly master-class for those lucky enough to see him in action. He read the game brilliantly, produced inch-perfect defence-splitting passes, and was from the great Scottish school of the 1930s. Furthermore, sleek Alex was a clinical finisher. In his first season, 1937/38, he rattled up 35 goals and in the succeeding campaign, managed another 22. Keeble was a good old-fashioned centre forward, one of the best of his era. An expert header of the ball, you could count on 30 goals a season, 10 at least from dashing winger Wright, so the goal potential of the team is enormous.

Several live candidates have been overlooked but by the narrowest of margins – Stan Foxall, Bobby Svarc and Mick Mahon especially.

So my team would line up thus – Walker, Fisher, Hall, Benny Fenton, Forbes, Kinsella, Lua Lua, Curry, Keeble, Cheyne and Wright. The manager would be Dick Graham and subs as follows – Ames, Cook, Bearryman, Bobby Hunt and Mahon. Have a little daydream over that squad and what it might achieve!

Historic List

Date: 28 August 1937   **Attendance:** 3,000 (Southern League)
Scoreline: Yeovil 3 (Halliday 3) United 0
Yeovil: Langford, Kingham, Burgess, Mann, Beswick, Hewes, Smith, Attley,
   Halliday, Kirk, Whyte.
United: Dunn, Fairchild, Wood, Collins, Leslie, Ritchie, Hodge, Pritchard,
   Smith, Cheyne, Crisp.

United's first-ever game and the daunting Huish slope proved too much. So too did dashing Dave Halliday, former Sunderland star, who was Yeovil's player manger. Their full name then was Yeovil and Petters United. The rail fare for the marathon trip was 13 shillings and Colchester's one moment of hope arrived when little George Crisp netted. The teams had lined up for the restart but the referee wiped out a goal for offside.

Date: 4 September 1937   **Attendance:** 11,000 (Southern League)
Scoreline: United 3 (Crisp, Wood, Cheyne) Ipswich Town 3 (Williams, Alsop,
   Perrett)
United: Dunn, Fairchild, Wood, Mayes, Leslie, Ritchie, Hodge, Pritchard,
   Smith, Cheyne, Crisp.
Ipswich Town: Houldsworth, Shufflebottom, Parry, Perrett, Rodger,
   McLuckie, Williams, Carter, Alsop, Bruce, Astill.

A week on and Colchester were engaged in their first-ever local derby. Professionalism had gripped East Anglia and somehow 11,000 crammed in the tree-fringed ground. U's had scored six in a midweek win over Bath and got three more in a thrill-a-minute affair against the old enemy. This time Crisp scored and it counted. Alex Cheyne and Alex Wood, after his first penalty had been saved, were the other marksmen in a dizzy encounter. Jack Williams and Gilbert Alsop put Town two up but U's came back to lead 3-2. Then George Perrett squared it from another penalty save and rebound.

Date: 5 February 1938   **Attendance:** 23,890 (Southern League)
Scoreline: Ipswich Town 3 (Astill, Perrett, Little) United 2 (Pritchard, Cheyne)
Ipswich Town: Sowerbutts, Shufflebottom, Parry, Perrett, Rodger, McLuckie, Williams, Bruce, Jones, Little, Astill.
United: Dunn, Fairchild, Wood, Baker, Leslie, Ritchie, Hodge, Pritchard, Fieldus, Cheyne, Barraclough.

The local derby of them all. Town and U's were battling it out at the top of the table and Portman Road had never seen such scenes – the crowd clung to girders, sat on stand roofs, and perched on the clock tower, and the game was like something out of *Roy of the Rovers*. Town scored first. Arthur Pritchard and Cheyne made it 2-1 and, with three minutes left, U's looked home and dry before allowing Ipswich to score twice at the death and it was a boob by 'keeper Ronnie Dunn that led to the winner. Poor Dunn was inconsolable for days.

Date: 10 January 1948   **Attendance:** 16,000 (FA Cup third round)
Scoreline: United 1 (Curry) Huddersfield Town 0
United: Wright, Kettle, Allen, Bearryman, Fenton, Brown, Hillman, Curry, Turner, Cutting, Cater.
Huddersfield Town: Hesford, Hayes, Barker, L. Smith, Hepplewhite, Boot, C. Smith, Glazzard, Wittingham, Doherty, Metcalfe.

The first big FA Cup sensation. Huddersfield, famed Peter Doherty and all, were cut down to size by Fenton's part-timers and it was no fluke. Fenton and Harry Bearryman shut Doherty out of the game, and dapper Bob Curry was the coolest player on the pitch when slotting the winner after Bob Hesford could only partially save a Bob Allen free-kick. Huddersfield tried all they knew but U's held on.

Date: 24 January 1948   **Attendance:** 17,000 (FA Cup fourth round)

Scoreline: United 3 (Curry 2, Cutting 1) Bradford Park Avenue 2 (Elliott, Ainsley)

United: Wright, Kettle, Allen, Bearryman, Fenton, Brown, Hillman, Curry, Turner, Cutting, Cater.

Bradford Park Avenue: Farr, Hepworth, Farrell, White, Greenwood, Deplidge, Smith, Henry, Ainsley, Downie, Elliott.

Billy Elliott, who had scored the dramatic winner that knocked out Arsenal in the previous round, gave Bradford an early lead but Bob Curry, in irresistible mood, scored twice, the second a goal worth framing – a top-speed move involving Len Cater and Fred Cutting. Bradford PA then superior to Bradford City, today's Division One outfit, squared thanks to a George Ainsley goal but little Cutting won it and Layer Road went mad.

Date: 7 February 1948   **Attendance:** 30,000 (FA Cup fifth round)

Scoreline: Blackpool 5 (Munro, McIntosh 2, Mortensen 2) United 0

Blackpool: Robinson, Shimwell, Stuart, Johnston, Hayward, Kelly, Matthews, Mortensen, McIntosh, Dick, Munro.

United: Wright, Kettle, Allen, Bearryman, Fenton, Brown, Hillman, Curry, Turner, Cutting, Cater.

Colchester fans invaded the famous old resort and lived it up, but the wonderful cup run was ended. A freakish second-minute opener by Alec Munro was the worst start possible but there was a fightback and it was half an hour before Jim McIntosh got the second. The rain teemed down and on the Bloomfield Road mud heap, we were entertained by the Stan Matthews-Stan Mortensen masterclass. They were unstoppable. Mortensen hit two and McIntosh made it five and that wizard of dribble Stanley put on a one man show.

Date: 19 August 1950   **Attendance:** 19,542 (Third Division South)

Scoreline: Gillingham 0, United 0

Gillingham: Gage, Marks, Lewin, Boswell, Kingsnorth, Collins, C. Burtenshaw, W. Burtenshaw, Russell, Ayres, Veck.

United: Wright, Kettle, Allen, Bearryman, Stewart, Elder, Jones, Curry, Turner, McKim, Church.

This was historic because it was Colchester's first ever Football League game. Close to 20,000, the Priestfield was packed. The mayor, Jack Andrews, sent a good luck message and the spotlight was full on, but this clash of old Southern League rivals proved a letdown. Maybe it was the big occasion and the considerable media attention but the game was dour and dull. Johnny Church went closest for U's and Harry Bearryman one of five 1948 survivors made a dramatic goal-line clearance. In the end it was about the right result and it started a sensational seven-match unbeaten opening run.

Date: 23 September 1950   **Attendance:** 13,483 (Third Division South)

Scoreline: United 2 (Cutting, Curry) Norwich City 3 (Hollis, Gavin 2)

United: Wright, Kettle, Allen, Bearryman, Stewart, Elder, Jones, Curry, Turner, Cutting, Keeble.

Norwich City: Nethercott, Duffy, Lewis, Pickwick, Foulkes, Ashman, Gavin, Kinsey, Hollis, Eyre, Docherty.

The first time U's met Norwich City and it was a typical five-goal thriller, but there was no disputing the Canaries' class. They were slick and sharp and ended the season as runners-up to Notts Forest. Jimmy Allen had Vic Keeble for the injured Johnny Church and another ex-Norwich player, Fred Cutting, was recalled. Eire international two-goal Johnny Gavin was Man of the Match. Roy Hollis got the other City goal. Cutting and Curry were U's marksmen and Bob Allen missed a penalty.

Date: 10 January 1953   **Attendance:** 16,547 (FA Cup third round)

Scoreline: Rotherham United 2 (Shaw 2) United 2 (McCurley 2)

Rotherham United: Quairney, Selkirk, Noble, Edwards, Gibson, Williams, Grainger, Guest, Shaw, Rawson, Rickett.

United: Wright, Harrison, Rookes, Bearryman, Stewart, Elder, Scott, Barlow, McCurley, McKim, Church.

A now largely forgotten cup tie that proved to be one of Kevin McCurley's best ever games. Rotherham were a Second Division power at the time with dazzling winger Jackie Grainger the danger man. Rotherham twice led and twice McCurley levelled, the U's attack in brilliant form. Augie Scott and Bert Barlow were outstanding. In the second half, George Wright saved a Grainger penalty. A relieved Jimmy Allen rushed on the field to shake his hand at the final whistle.

Date: 15 January 1953   **Attendance:** 8,991 (FA Cup third round replay)

Scoreline: United 0 Rotherham United 2 (Shaw, Rawson)

United: Wright, Harrison, Rookes, Bearryman, Stewart, Elder, Scot, Barlow, McCurley, McKim, Church.

Rotherham United: Quairney, Selkirk, Noble, Edwards, B. Williams, D. Williams, Grainger, Guest, Shaw, Rawson, Rickett.

United departed from the cup and lost the chance of a tilt at Newcastle United on a murky misty day. A remarkable near-9,000 crowd for a Thursday afternoon game indicated considerable work absenteeism. They witnessed a dour unspectacular struggle. McCurley had one near-miss and then Jack Shaw and Colin Rawson goals sealed a comfortable win.

Date: 16 February 1957   **Attendance:** 18,559 (Third Division South)

Scoreline: United 0 Ipswich Town 0

United: Ames, Fisher, Fowler, Fenton, Milligan, Dale, Williams, Hill, McCurley, Plant, Wright.

Ipswich Town: Bailey, Carberry, Malcolm, Myles, Rees, Elsworthy, Reed, Millward, Garneys, Phillips, Leadbetter.

The most titanic Colchester-Ipswich contest of them all. This was the U's heartbreak near-miss promotion season. Both teams were in the running and Layer Road had never seen such crowd scenes – the gates shut with thousands outside. Colchester made the running and should have won, but a Benny Fenton penalty was brilliantly saved by Roy Bailey. Town suffered from having crack-shot Ted Phillips crocked early on – after a Fenton tackle! And Peter Wright was brilliant, giving Larry Carberry the runaround. But Town, who won promotion by one point, hung on.

Date: 24 January 1959   **Attendance:** 16,000 (FA Cup fourth round)

Scoreline: United 2 (Langman, Evans) Arsenal 2 (Groves)

United: Ames, Fisher, Fowler, Parker, Milligan, Hammond, Blake, McCleod, Langman, Evans, Wright.

Arsenal: Kelsey, Wills, D. Evans, Ward, Docherty, Bowen, Clapton, Groves, Herd, Bloomfield, Henderson.

A memorable tie. Arsenal, leading the First Division at the time, were so surprised by Colchester's quality football. Peter Wright and Tommy Williams gave their backs the complete runaround. The match was on a knife edge but Danny Clapton looked to have won it before two late goals thrilled the crowd. Big Neil Langman charged down the middle to cut the lead and John Evans brought the house down with the equaliser. The Gunners hung on by the skin of their teeth in a frantic finale.

Date: 28 January 1959   Attendance: 62,686 (FA Cup fourth round replay)
Scoreline: Arsenal 4 (Herd 2, Julians, Evans 2) United 0
Arsenal: Kelsey, Wills, Evans, Ward, Docherty, Bowen, Clapton, Groves, Herd, Julians, Henderson.
United: Same as in first game.

The replay was a complete turnaround. On a chaotic night of freezing fog and an Underground failure, the Highbury gates were locked. What transpired on the pitch broke Colchester hearts. Wearing special footwear, the Gunners dominated it and, for much of the game, it was Percy Ames taking on Arsenal single-handedly. The gate remains the biggest involving a Colchester team and the reward a share of £10,035 receipts.

Date: 10 October 1960   **Attendance:** 9,130 (League Cup first round)
Scoreline: United 4 (King 2, Williams, Wright) Newcastle United 1 (Neale)
United: Ames, Rumney, Fowler, Harris, Milligan, R.M. Hunt, Williams, McLeod, King, Hill, Wright.
Newcastle United: Harvey, Keith, McMicheal, Neale, Heslop, Duton, Wilson, Woods, White, Allchurch, Mitten.

A shock result, the more remarkable in that Colchester were on a gloomy run and it was relegation season, but they turned it on with style to beat the powerful Newcastle side, Ivor Allchurch and all, out of sight. It was the inauguration of the Football League Cup and the recalled Sammy McLeod and Bobby Hill plotted a great victory. A debut night too that Trevor Harris will always remember.

Date: 25 September 1963   **Attendance:** 7,772 (League Cup first round)

Scoreline: United 5 (Grice, R.R. Hunt (pen), King, Stark 2) Fulham 3 (Key, Metchick 2)

United: Ramage, Forbes, Woods, McCrohan, Rutter, R.M. Hunt, Grice, R.R. Hunt, King, Stark, Wright.

Fulham: Townsend, Cohen, Langley, Mullery, Keetch, Robson, Key, Metchick, Cook, Haynes, Leggett.

The night the great Johnny Haynes came to town and left stunned by a superlative Colchester display. Alan Mullery, George Cohen and Bobby Robson were other big names in a Fulham side that had no answer to U's slick attacking. Martyn King, ever the man for the big occasion, was a shining light. So too was the two-goal Billy Stark.

Date: 27 January 1968   **Attendance:** 15,981 (FA Cup third round)

Scoreline: United 1 (Stratton) West Brom 1 (Brown)

United: Adams, Mochan, Hall, Trevis, Forbes, Blackwood, Price, Mansfield, Stratton, McKechnie, Martin.

West Brom: Osborne, Colquhoun, Williams, Brown, Talbut, Fraser, Krzywicki, Kaye, Astle, Hope, Clark.

Albion escaped with a replay by the skin of their teeth and this was U's best display under Neil Franklin. Reg Stratton opened the scoring and the bar robbed him of a second. A harsh penalty decision allowed Tony Brown to level and it was the great escape again when John Mansfield netted near time only for a goal to be ruled out for hands.

Date: 31 January 1968   **Attendance:** 40,008 (FA Cup third round replay)

Scoreline: West Brom 4 (Kaye, Astle 2, Clark) United 0

West Brom: Shepherd, Colquhoun, Williams, Brown, Talbut, Fraser, Lovett, Kaye, Astle, Hope, Clark.

United: Adams, Mochan, Hall, Trevis, Forbes, Blackwood, Price, Mansfield, Stratton, Bullock, Martin.

Anti-climax at the Hawthorns. One wondered why a replay was necessary as Albion, making changes after their let off, strolled to victory and went all the way to Wembley. Jeff Astle spearheaded their attack, scoring twice. U's had their fair share of the second half but were never in the hunt.

Date: 13 February 1971   **Attendance:** 16,000 (FA Cup fifth round)

Scoreline: United 3 (Crawford 2, Simmons) Leeds United 2 (Hunter, Giles)

United: Smith, Cram, Hall, Gilchrist, Garvey, Kurila, Lewis, Simmons, Mahon, Crawford, Gibbs.

Leeds United: Sprake, Reaney, Cooper, Bates, Charlton, Hunter, Lorimer, Clarke, Jones, Giles, Madeley.

This still remains the biggest cup shock of all time. Ray Crawford, playing the game of his life, scored twice, once while laying on his bottom. When Dave Simmons made it 3-0, we thought we were dreaming. It was a master display of tactics and kidology against the top team in Europe. Norman Hunter and Johnny Giles cut it back to 3-2 and a marvel save by Graham Smith was the final thrill.

Date: 6 March 1971   **Attendance:** 53,028 (FA Cup sixth round)

Scoreline: Everton 5 (Kendall 2, Royle, Husband, Ball) United 0

Everton: Rankin, Wright, Newton, Kendall, Kenyon, Harvey, Husband, Ball, Royle, Hurst, Morrissey.

United: Smith, Cram, Hall, Gilchrist, Garvey, Kurila, Lewis, Simmons, Crawford, Mahon, Gibbs.

The end of the road at a packed Goodison Park. For twenty minutes, U's were a threat, Crawford going close but four quick goals won the day. Even when Colchester battled for a consolation they were out of luck, Gibbs hitting a post and Lewis having a shot cleared. Alan Ball wrapped it up with a fifth goal but United went off the field to a standing ovation.

Date: 7 August 1971   **Attendance:** 18,487 (Watney Cup final)

Scoreline: West Brom 4 (Cantello, Astle 2, Hope) United 4 (Mahon 2, Simmons, Lewis (pen)). Colchester won 4-3 on penalties

West Brom: Cumbes, Hughes, Wilson, Cantello, Wile, Kaye, Suggett, Brown, Astle, Hope, Hartford.

United: Smith, Cram, Hall, Gilchrist, Garvey, Burgess, Bloss, Lewis, Gibbs, Simmons, Mahon.

The historic Watney Cup triumph, U's winning after a thrilling penalty shoot-out, teenager Phil Bloss stroking home the vital kick with great composure. The match had been a see-saw thriller. U's led but then trailed 3-2. They came back to go in front 4-3 before a last-ditch Jeff Astle equaliser. Millions watched afterwards on *Match of the Day*.

Date: 13 November 1974   **Attendance:** 9,615 (League Cup fourth round)
Scoreline: United 0 Southampton 0
United: Walker, A. Smith, Bunkell, Leslie, Harford, Dominey, Thomas, Svarc,
   Froggatt, Lindsay, Cook.
Southampton: Turner, McCarthy, Mills, Fisher, Bennett, Steele, Stokes, Channon,
   Osgood, Peach, Gilchrist.

Southampton, valued at £500,000, were fortunate to escape with a replay on a wild rain-swept night. U's had the better of a grim struggle and went close in an exciting finale as Colchester kept going a good run that had seen them dispose of Oxford, Southend and Carlisle.

Date: 25 November 1974   **Attendance:** 11,492 (League Cup fourth round replay)
Scoreline: Southampton 0 United 1 (Dominey)
Southampton: Turner, McCarthy, Mills, Fisher, Bennett, Steele, Stokes, Channon,
   McCleod, Peach, Gilchrist.
United: Walker, Cook, A. Smith, Leslie, Harford, Dominey, Thomas, Svarc,
   Froggatt, Lindsay, Bunkell.

A classic victory always remembered for the save of Mike Walker's career – a one-handed tip over from a Mike Channon rocket free-kick. Colchester, on a thrill-packed Dell night, shocked the crowd when eighteen-year-old Barry Dominey headed the winner from Steve Leslie's free-kick. Saints lacked suspended Peter Osgood but could have no complaints.

Date: 3 December 1974   **Attendance:** 11,871 (League Cup fifth round)
Scoreline: United 1 (Froggatt) Aston Villa 2 (Little, Graydon)
United: Walker, Cook, Packer, Leslie, Harford, Dominey, Thomas, Svarc, Froggatt,
   Lindsay, Bunkell.
Villa: Cumbes, Robson, Aitken, Ross, Nicholl, Brown, Graydon, Little, Morgan,
   Hamilton, Carrodus.

The end of the road at last and it was a rather anti-climactic affair. U's just could not compete with a well-organised Villa, making a first-ever Layer Road appearance. An early goal by Brian Little virtually settled it and Ray Graydon sealed the issue before a late John Froggatt consolation. The gate of under 12,000 was cruelly disappointing considering a two-legged semi-final was within touching distance.

Date: 20 February 1979   **Attendance:** 13,171 (FA Cup fifth round)

Scoreline: United 0 Manchester United 1 (J. Greenhoff)

United: Walker, Cook, Wright, Hodge, Wignall, Dowman, Packer, Foley, Dyer, Lee, Allison.

Manchester United: Bailey, B. Greenhoff, Albiston, McIlroy, McQueen, Buchan, Coppell, J. Greenhoff, Ritchie, Macari, Thomas.

The first ever Manchester United visit to Layer Road and they only just made it thanks to a late Jim Greenhoff goal. Earlier, U's had certainly had their moments and Trevor Lee was unlucky when his shot was cleared off the line. Even then, a replay beckoned and Colchester were unlucky losers. It was the first time a U's side had been beaten at home by a First Division outfit.

Date: 8 November 1983   **Attendance:** 13,031 (League Cup third round)

Scoreline: United 0 Manchester United 2 (McQueen, Moses)

United: Chamberlain, Cook, Farrell, Hadley, Wignall, Houston, Leslie, Osborne, Bowen, Adcock, Hubbick, Sub – Groves.

Manchester United: Bailey, Duxbury, Albiston, Wilkins, Moran, McQueen, Robson, Moses, Stapleton, Whiteside, Graham, Sub – Macari.

The Red Devils' second visit in the then Milk Cup. It ended in a straight-forward win after an early scare when Gordon McQueen cleared off the line and then scored at the other end. It as all over bar the shouting when a classic move saw Bryan Robson put Remi Moses through for the clincher. Colchester never stopped battling but class told in the end.

Date: 10 May 1991   **Attendance:** 27,806 (FA Trophy final, Wembley)

Scoreline: United 3 (Masters, Smith, McGavin) Witton Albion 1 (Lutkevitch)

United: Barrett, Donald, Roberts, Kinsella, English, Martin, Cook, Masters, McDonough, McGavin, Smith.

Witton Albion: Mason, Halliday, Coathup, McNellis, Connor, Anderson, Thomas, Rose, Alford, Grimshaw, Lutkevitch.

Colchester's first-ever Wembley appearance and a great victory to bring off the Conference – Trophy double. A triumph for Roy McDonough and his merry men and they never looked back after an early goal from popular Yank Mike Masters. Nicky Smith made it two following a classic move and after a feisty Albion had pulled one back, Steve McGavin calmly slotted a third. The only blot on the big day was the harsh sending off of Jason Cook.

Date: 20 April 1997   **Attendance:** 45,077 (Auto Windscreen final, Wembley)

Scoreline: United 0 Carlisle United 0 (Carlisle won on penalty shoot-out)

United: Emberson, Dunne, Greene, Cawley, Gibbs, Abrahams, Gregory, Whitton, Wilkins, Sale, Adcock. Subs: Fry, Duguid, Locke.

Carlisle United: Caig, Delap, Archdeacon, Walling, Varty, Pounewatchy, Peacock, Conway, Smart, Hayward, Aspinall. Subs: Thomas, Jansen, Hooper.

A nail-biting penalty shoot out saw U's go down 4–3 in heartbreaking fashion. They had matched Carlisle in every department in normal and extra time in a dourly contested final watched by an especially large crowd. Joe Dunne was within inches of winning it before the ninety minutes were up when he fired just over. Karl Duguid and Peter Cawley missed the vital spot-kicks.

Date: 22 May 1998   **Attendance:** 19,486 (Div. 3 play-off final, Wembley)

Scoreline: United 1 (D. Gregory, pen) Torquay United 0

United: Emberson, Dunne, Greene, Wilkins, Betts, Skelton, Buckle, D. Gregory, Forbes, N. Gregory, Sale. Subs: Duguid, Lock, Abrahams.

Torquay United: Gregg, Gurney, Gittens, Robinson, Watson, Gibbs, McCall, Clayton, Leadbitter, Jack, McFarlane. Subs: Beadeau, Thomas, Hill.

A quick Wembley return for manager Steve Wignall and a glory night with the winning of promotion to Division Two. It was far from a classic game but U's were always just that better and deserving victors even though the winner was from the penalty spot. The scoring hero was all-purpose David Gregory, one of the success stories of the season. He finished leading scorer.

It's a Fact

* Colchester United have had three lady secretaries – Betty Scott, Dee Elwood and currently Marie Partner.

* *Highest scoring Colchester victories – 9-1 v. Bradford City in 1961, 8-2 v. Stockport County in 1958.*

* Biggest home attendance – 19,072 *v.* Reading FA Cup 1948, League 18,559 *v.* Ipswich 1957.

* *Biggest cup wins – 7-1 v. Woodford Town 1950, 7-1 v. Yeovil 1958. Both away.*

* Four Colchester United managers who were goalkeepers – Ted Davis, Dick Graham, Mike Walker, Jock Wallace.

* *Hat-tricks on debut – Vic Keeble v. Bedford 1947, Ted Phillips v. Barnsley 1965.*

* Longest-serving manager – Benny Fenton, February 1955 to November 1963.

* *Shortest-serving manager – Ron Meades 11 June to 15 June 1953.*

* Most goals in a season – Bobby Hunt, 39 in 1961/62.

* *Most goals – Martyn King 132.*

* Biggest gate in away match – 62,686 *v.* Arsenal FA Cup 1959.

* *Unbeaten at home – Third Division (South), 1956/57.*

* Best-ever League season – third in Third Division (South) 1956/57.

* *Wembley three times – FA Trophy v. Whitton 1992. Autoglass final v. Carlisle 1997 and Division Three play-off final v. Torquay 1998.*

* Quickest Colchester goal – Martyn King *v.* Norwich City, twenty-four seconds, 1960.

* *Record gate for friendly – 12,306* v. *Ipswich Town, 1948*

* Record gate for away friendly – 35,000 *v.* Arsenal at Highbury, 1948.

* *Ex-Colchester United players appearing in the World Cup 2002 – Mark Kinsella and Efe Sodje.*

* Best FA Cup run – sixth round 1970.

* *Teams never met in League or Cup – Chelsea, Leicester City, Tottenham Hotspur, Bolton, Liverpool, Sunderland, West Ham and Boston United.*

Epilogue

Season 2003/04, while action-packed, did not quite completely satisfy. After so much early promise, there was no play-off prize. The long-overdue FA Cup run was a factor proving an obvious distraction as did the LDV Vans Trophy. Another disappointment here, for U's were hot favourites to lift this cup and pick up some lottery-type cash. Unaccountably, Southend upset the apple cart.

Although a little bemused at times by some of his team selections, I like Phil Parkinson, sound, solid and popular with players and fans alike – a manager in the modern idiom and chairman Peter Heard chose well.

Something Parkinson has come up with is the rarity for Colchester of four scoring players: Scott McGleish, Wayne Andrews, Craig Fagan and Rowan Vine who, between them, totted up more than 50 goals.

Colchester games were inconsistent. The squad kept blowing hot and cold but when at their best, they compared favourably to what I call the 'good old black and white days'. Mind you, from the press box, I so often see ace phantoms from the past parading their skills and more than once sigh for ten minutes of a Sammy McCleod or a Bobby Hill. A player to put his foot on the ball and exercise some control over a game lost to harum-scarum pace, but then I am a devout nostalgia buff.

Three players currently catching my eye are Fagan, Joe Keith and the local lad Greg Halford. Fagan is young with some dazzling skills but must overcome a not-too-good disciplinary record. I still find it amazing that

Birmingham City let him go so readily. Fagan could have a terrific future and is hungry for the big time. His hat-trick game against Notts County was one of the season's highlights.

I have always liked Keith for his skills and confidence – a player who goes at a defence, taking players on and scoring some notable goals for full measure.

Halford, a stripling of a lad, is a defender who looks to have everything and could be a prize player of the future. He looks like a natural and has come up through the ranks.

Depressingly, Layer Road gates still hover around the 3,500 mark although there was some very good support for away trips in the FA Cup run, and I'm sure there would have been a mass exodus to Cardiff if the LDV Vans final had become reality, but it's the bread-and-butter League fare that demands better support.

It's hard to imagine, but 3,000 was the average gate for Colchester reserve games in the late 1940s and early 1950s. In 1948/49, there were 5,691 for a game against Chelmsford City reserves and 5,377 when Spurs A came to town. But this was of course another era when life was more laid-back and there were few counter-attractions. I recall midweek games with 5.30 p.m. kick-offs and hordes of fans streaming out of factories and shops ignoring tea and heading hell-bent for Layer Road, the majority by bicycle.

I was there in 1938 when somehow 17,584 people crammed in Layer Road for the Colchester Challenge Cup showpiece between Arsenal and Wolves when ringside seating meant one could have reached out and touched a young Denis Compton who paraded his talents that memorable night.

In 1960 for a Norwich City local derby, there was a 13,053 attendance – and there hasn't been a League gate since to reach those heights and nor will there ever be. When – or should we say if – the new Cuckoo Farm all-seat stadium becomes reality, 10,000 will be the capacity.

That's why Colchester United's past seems so fascinating and histori-cally important. But although the modern game has its detractors, there are good points and change is inevitable. Colchester United, with a wise and prudent chairman, has moved well with the times.

I have forgotten down the years the number of times I edited and wrote most of the club programme. Today's splendid glossy effort is the work of media manager Matt Hudson, and his assistant Colin Wood leaves all other earlier efforts in the shade, modern day innovations obviously a help. It's a match day magazine of near-Premiership standard.

There are many things I miss – a packed stand behind the Layer Road end where so many historic goals have been scored. It invariably exuded so much fervour and excitement and was worth a goal start every time U's attacked that end. Now it's reserved for visiting supporters and is usually half empty.

I miss the excited buzz on the long-since-gone open Spion Kop end and thrilling wing-play from the likes of Peter Wright, prince of flank men and the utterly devastating Brian Hall, who was one of the pioneers of wing-back play.

Sadly, Brian is one of many great favourites who have passed on in recent months. He was a great character who was just a run of the mill left-winger signed from Mansfield Town until Dick Graham switched him to full-back. It was an inspired move and Brian with that electric burst of pace was awe-inspiring. I am of the view that he would today be a Premiership performer as would have been Vic Keeble, Wright and the enigmatical but brilliant Martyn King.

Apart from Hall, we have lost among others Len Cater, Cecil Allan, Bert Barlow, Mike Grice, Andy Brown and Bill Bower. Cater, in many ways, was a quintessential 1930s, 1940s player who had the best of several worlds. Initially an amateur, Len, or Spud as he was universally known, turned professional at a time when many thought his career over. Ted Fenton seemed to inspire Len and he was a leading light in the famed 1948 FA Cup run. Len was short and stocky but possessed courage aplenty along with wing skills including an exquisite cross, and most importantly, he was cockily confident and bouncingly full of himself. He seemed to go on forever. Cecil Allan was never a great player but a steady full-back in the pre-war Southern League days and a most charming Irishman with a lilting voice to match. Bert Barlow but for the intervention of war would have achieved much more. He was originally of the old baggy shorts brigade, an FA Cup winner with Portsmouth in 1939, that medal one of his most cherished possessions. Jack Butler signed him in the twilight of his career when he was thirty-two and although he played only 67 U's games, he holds a supreme place in the all-time gallery of greats.

Also sadly missed will be sports writer of many years on U's deeds, Arthur Wood, who represented the *Essex County Standard* and *Colchester Gazette*. Arthur, a true Scot, was the perfect gentleman and a quality writer with many a witticism as when he penned of Sammy McLeod, 'He could make a football talk, with a Scottish accent of course.'

Soccer has seen so many changes although a few things stay the same. Starry-eyed kids today experience the same tug of excitement over watching Karl Duguid and Wayne Andrews as did their 1950 counterparts in cheering on Kevin McCurley and Sammy McLeod.

There is still a mascot, Eddie the Eagle, where before there was The Umbrella Man, and Taffy, and Whisky the dog who once went to Aldershot on a Christmas morning. When it comes to managers, Phil Parkinson is as revered as was Jimmy Allen.

But generally the game is barely recognisable. Two points for a win, no subs, no play-offs, no penalty shoot-outs. No floodlights and no Sunday football, although clubs did play on Christmas Day morning. There was most significantly no television or big money to dictate when and where matches should be played and the game too was uncomplicated with full-backs, wing halves, inside forwards and wingers. Now we are weighed down with tactics and a more sophisticated approach.

Crowds then were bigger. The tragic events of Hillsborough and Valley Parade have rightly led to a strict safety code. For all that, it remains a mystery to me why there is a 7,500 Layer Road limit today when in 1938, when it was antiquated by comparison, more then 17,000 watched in complete security, if not comfort. Was the game as such better in the 1930s, '40s and '50s? If only there were video films to make comparisons. We shall never know.

My judgement of the 1938/39 Southern League championship side is clouded by a schoolboy's adoration and, through those young admiring eyes, all the U's players were lionised. Spectators and players were closer together even at First Division level. With the advent of mega wages, the gap has grown and keeps growing. Spectators enjoyed the game more in a laid-back manner. I always recollect after the 1948 cup wins over Huddersfield and Bradford, bands of happy fans linked arm in arm, the width of Butt road singing their way back to town. Of course in 1937 when professionalism swept East Anglia, it was a novelty. For many a year there had been a nondescript amateur Colchester Town playing before a handful of spectators. Now a side packed with well-known League professionals were representing the town with marked success.

The first season was encouraging and U's won the Southern League Cup. The second campaign saw enthusiasm intensify and Colchester were Southern League Champions. I'm convinced that but for the intervention of war they would have rapidly followed Ipswich into the Football League.

I liked the way the *East Anglian Daily Times* in the quaint sports journalistic style of the day heralded professionalism. In the report of the 3-3 draw against Ipswich they said, 'If any of the Colchester and district Saturday public are not satisfied with the introduction of professional football to north-east Essex, they are very hard to please. A better send off could hardly have been hoped for by those who, in the face of adverse criticism and even opposition, carried out the spadework which led to the formation.' The U's players were feted wherever they went. Memories flood back of the team invited by the Playhouse cinema to see a film. They were seated in a private box and during the interval the spotlight turned on them and amid cheers they took a bow.

Crowds then included a fair number of women supporters and plenty of kids. Nearly all wore rosettes and supporters club badges with bars for each succeeding season. Most men had shiny brylcreamed hair or sported caps or trilbies. Youngsters were invariably given prime vantage points and there was a general air of good humour, everyone wearing a smile.

Several players had nicknames. Central defender George Leslie, a solid figure who later became a policeman, was The Rock. Midfielder George Smith, a workmanlike artisan signed from Bath City, was dubbed Farmer Smith, and diminutive left-winger George Crisp was 'wee Georgie'.

It's odd. In those days, pre-season games were invariably Probables *v.* Possibles which in effect was the likely first team against the reserves. Then there were the newspaper reports of players signed which often mentioned that the performer concerned was a teetotaller and non-smoker. Great importance was given if they were abstainers but in truth they were in the minority.

The Colchester team of 1937 were all smokers with the exception of full-back Alex Wood and, it is said that George Leslie smoked a pipe containing a most pungent tobacco which led to him being banished to the corridor during an away journey. This was the trip to Yeovil for the first ever pro-match when it was also reputed that the players got through four packets of twenty cigarettes on the outward journey. The return rail fare to Yeovil was thirteen shillings and sixpence. Many professionals were indeed habitual smokers and there is a famous memorabilia photo of pre-war Ipswich players in the dressing room baths with at least four of them smoking cigarettes.

U's in these pre-war days had their own song. Cinema organist Tommy Walker wrote, 'Up the U's the good old white and blues' and it proved quite a hit. It was performed with great gusto on match days. Layer Road was primitive but buzzed with excitement. Pre-kick-off music usually comprised rousing Sousa marches and the team ran out to the Post Horn Gallop. A big feature was a half-time scoreboard – no scores over the tannoy then – and one needed a programme for the key.

The manager Ted Davis was dapper and dynamic. He had been a goal-keeper with Huddersfield Town and then managed Bath City. Davis was something to the small club that George Allison was to Arsenal, and very much an entrepreneur. For example, he organised the Colchester Challenge Cup showpieces between Arsenal and Wolves – that was the match that drew that 17,000 witnessed – and the following season with Arsenal and Spurs. There was ringside seating for the very first time for Arsenal and Wolves. It was a great novelty with two of the country's leading sides on show.

When Arsenal and Spurs played, there was a touch of Wembley when song-leader Mr T. Ratcliffe of the *News Chronicle* conducted pre-kick-off community singing.

Davis was full of ideas and didn't miss a trick. I remember a friendly arranged against Charlton Athletic being put in doubt by the sudden arrival of snow. In those non-TV days, communication was more difficult but having the pitch cleared and ready for play, Davis organised cars to tour the town with loudspeaker hailers announcing that the match was on.

As a manager, Davis was not over popular in that he poached away a lot of players from their clubs and had few scruples, but he signed well and often and was always looking to strengthen the side. In mid-season he signed a goalkeeper, Fred Youngs, an RAF serviceman stationed at Martlesham. Bill Light, the regular 'keeper who had been close to an England cap when with West Brom, was in brilliant form but Davis felt he needed cover and Youngs in fact played in some vital games.

Then there was the enlistment of popular Harwich and Parkeston amateur striker, Tully Day. Colchester were prolific scorers at the time, but Davis thought there was a case for more firepower and the added advantage was that colourful Day proved to be a crowd-puller.

Colchester's number one player by far was dapper Alex Cheyne, the former Chelsea Scottish ace, a supreme ball artist. There was no way he should have been playing non-League but Davis induced him to Layer Road and there's little doubt Cheyne was on top money. He was also a prolific scorer, not the number one marksman but for all that, 22 goals in 42 games in 1938/39 was high consistency.

Davis also pirated slick winger Jackie Hodge from Luton Town and again cash was almost certainly the key as Hodge, brilliant on his day, had attracted Arsenal and other top clubs. Luton were furious when he went non-League. Davis scored also by selling players – goalkeeper Ted Platt and full-back Cliff Fairchild to Arsenal and inside forward Reg Smith to Wolves.

Other popular players include prolific scoring centre forward Arthur Prichard. He had little finesse but plenty of bustle and totted up a remarkable 76 goals in two seasons. Arthur was a lion-hearted Welshman and was best summed up by a clever *News Chronicle* cartoonist Mercer whose words accompanying his brilliant caricature of a U's *v.* Ilford FA Cup tie read, 'with a young fellah named Pritchard at centre-forward, Colchester beat Ilford. There was none of the pretty stuff about Mr Prichard, no sir. He attacked with everything except a smoke screen or depth charges putting all he had into his job – we think Mr Pritchard must have had the idea he was a tank. Once a dog invaded the pitch – but it was intelligent enough to realise that no dog could ever have its day with a Pritchard knocking around.'

Classier acts were ex-Norwich men, full-back Alf Worton and midfielder Roy Morris, but not every Davis signing turned up trumps. He captured Ernie Matthews to a hail of trumpets. Matthews was a star turn up north with Bury. He had a big reputation and was also an ace sprinter but after scoring on his debut, played only 7 games and spent nearly all his time in the reserves.

Season 1938/39 was an exhausting marathon. Can you believe that 69 matches in all were played and 48 were won and 172 goals scored! Morris played all 69 and was reputed to have thrown down his boots after the last match exclaiming, 'They are like me, buggered!' I find an East Anglian *Daily Times* report amusing. They recorded that Worton missed only one of the 69 games – against Norwich reserves when he was rested!'

The Southern League was a powerful combination including the reserve sides of several League clubs – there were ten second elevens in 1939 – who shuttled players to and fro so that U's often faced strong opposition. Norwich City, with their then very vivid yellow and green quartered shirts were a case in point. Arsenal 'A', the Gunners third team were a powerful outfit frequently bristling with big names.

The Saturday pilgrimage to Layer Road continued to amaze with the local bus shuttle service from town a boon. The 1938/39 season was just one big success story and there was more than one 10,000 crowd, a sure-fire draw, always the Good Friday clash with Guildford City, the number one rivals in U's title push. Easter was inevitably a hectic exciting soccer holiday and teams were also in action on Easter Saturday and Easter Monday – three games in four days.

Guildford had been champions in 1937/38 and were right in contention up to the last match of the season. U's were at Portman Road facing a strong Ipswich Town reserves side and a point would have been enough. As it was they won 3-2 and the winner always sticks in my mind. Len Astill, a fleet-footed left-winger who had been with Ipswich a year earlier scored the vital goal with a shot so powerful the ball rebounded from a goal stanchion thirty yards into play. It all happened so quickly that many spectators thought Astill had hit the bar.

The boyish-faced Astill had been with Blackburn Rovers and it's a mystery how this skilled schoolboy international never made the top stage. But that could have been said of several of Davis's remarkable side that had one unbeaten run of 13 games without defeat. That last game at Portman Road drew a crowd of 12,014 people – an astonishing attendance for a reserve match. Town had in the action the erstwhile George Perrett, often the scourge of Colchester in the past, and Town, as always, made it a tight affair.

In those days, there was no pyramid system with automatic promotion as there is now with the Conference. Had there been, that very Guildford side would have been in the League, for they were twice champions in the 1930s. They were always U's biggest threat and had a side with a predominantly Scottish flavour and a dangerous right-winger with the odd name

Bytheway! The biggest chopping blocks for Colchester were invariably poor old Newport County reserves who were thrashed 8-0 and 7-0 in successive seasons.

The bogey side had to be Plymouth Argyle reserves, the only team to win a match at Layer Road in two seasons. They did so in 1937/38 and again in 1938/39 which underlines what a fortress Layer Road was those far-off days.

It's odd. These days it's definitely not the case. Frances Ponder and I were discussing the point the other day and he is firmly of the view that the positioning of visiting supporters behind the Layer Road end is a big factor. When it was 100 per cent full by noisy home fans, U's seemed a much more potent force. There is certainly something to be said for the theory.

Something that U's missed out on was some FA Cup excitement and they certainly had the side that could well have knocked over a Third Division outfit. In the fourth qualifying round hopes were high as Ilford, crack amateurs of the day, were drawn at home. In earlier years, Ilford would have made mincemeat of the old Colchester Town, but they were well-beaten and U's were optimistic of further progress when away to unfancied Folkestone who delivered the knockout blow at Cheriton Park.

The cup headlines were in fact collared by Chelmsford City who had just joined the professional bandwagon and reached the fourth round, going out to Birmingham, 6-0. The novelty and allure of professionalism swept East Anglia and there were whispers that Lowestoft and Yarmouth might burn their amateur boats. But of course it never happened.

Looking back, one thinks of those proud Southern League clubs who are now no more – the delightfully-named Tunbridge Wells Rangers, Guildford City and Barry Town. But romantically, over sixty years on, Colchester will have met up again with Cheltenham Town after their elevation to Division Two. Their Whaddon Road ground remains, much revamped it goes without saying.

Layer Road has altered drastically too. After the war, the terracing that flanked the grandstand was covered and eventually the new £170,000 stand replaced the old Spion Kop. In the 1940s it had looked some sight packed to the limits, but it had long since become run down and an eyesore.

But let's think of the new season, the sixty-seventh as professionals and there is general optimism that 2004/05 could at last be a promotion year, after a campaign of great promise with many a highlight – the tremendous draw at Coventry and the replay win – the resilience in defeat at Bramall Lane and a notable double over Sheffield Wednesday.

It turned out to be the best Division Two season ever both points-wise and position-wise. We must remember of course that Coca-Cola Football League One is in fact only on a par with the old Second Division but let's hope the Parkinson show can surpass Benny Fenton's 1956/57 best-ever near-miss season. And hope too that the new stadium finally becomes reality and that we don't finish up in cloud cuckoo land instead!